# Dictionary of Confusable Words

# Dictionary of Confusable Words

**Harmik Vaishnav**

PRABHAT
PRAKASHAN

*Published by*
**PRABHAT PRAKASHAN PVT. LTD.**
4/19 Asaf Ali Road,
New Delhi-110 002 (INDIA)
e-mail: prabhatbooks@gmail.com

ISBN 978-93-5048-186-8
**DICTIONARY OF CONFUSABLE WORDS**
*by* Harmik Vaishnav



*Edition*
2025

*Price*
₹ 450.00 (Rupees Four Hundred Fifty only)

*Printed at*
Narula Printers, Delhi

# Author's Note

Spellings and pronunciation are very important in English language. One of the characteristics of this language is that there are many words with a slight change in spelling, similar pronunciation but different meanings. Such words are called homonyms or homophones.

In this book, many groups of such words are given along with sentences for explanation of the difference of meanings. This will help in understanding the language better and make the usages of the words smooth. It also shows that a spelling error can change the meaning of the word and hence the sentence to a great extent.

This book will be useful to understand the right use of word. The usage is explained with a sentence for understanding. It will be useful to students; aspirants of competitive exams, professionals and of course the lovers of English language.

**—Harmik Vaishnav**

# Contents

# A

1 **Abase** Degrade

*The boss **abased** his subordinates in the meeting.*

**Abash** Embarrass

The father was **abashed** due to his son's behaviour in the college.

2 **Abbe** Priest

*I met an old abbe in the church yesterday and learnt about religion from him.*

**Ebb** Low tide

The moon controls **ebb** and tide in the sea.

3 **Abode** Dwelling-place

*That den is the **abode** of a ferocious lion.*

**Adobe** Sun-dried brick

In summer, the **adobe** production increases.

4 **Abject** Miserable

*The **abject** condition of the flood victims was painful to us.*

**Object** Thing, oppose

Why do you **object** his views?

Is this an **object** for play?

5 **Able** Capable
*That wonder boy is **able** to operate big machines at this tender age.*
**Amble** Move at easy speed
The monkey can **amble** among trees.

6 **Abroad** Go to other country
*I am going **abroad** as a representative of our company.*
**Aboard** On the ship
There were hundreds of passengers **aboard** the Titanic when it sank.

7 **Absorb** Include, pull
*Cotton **absorbs** water easily.*
**Adsorb** Hold to surface
Water **adsorbs** cork.

8 **Abstract** Summary, not concrete
*I am reading the **abstract** of a novel. Emotion is an abstract thing.*
**Extract** Remove
I **extracted** juice from the lemon.

9 **Accede** Agree
*The customer did not **accede** to our offer of discount.*
**Exceed** To be greater than
Rahul **exceeded** his father in income.

10 **Accent** Mode of pronunciations
*The British **accent** is very different from American accent.*
**Ascent** Climb-up
The **ascent** was difficult because of the slippery surface.
**Assent** Agree
Will your parents **assent** to marriage with her?

11 **Accept** To receive anything
*I am glad that you **accepted** my invitation.*
**Except** Excluding
**Except** you, all the members were present in the meeting.
**Expect** To hope
The managing director **expects** all the officers to reach the office by 10.00 a.m.

12 **Access** Approach
*Mr. Khan has a good **access** to the domestic market.*
**Excess** More than due
Anything in **excess** is not good.

13 **Accomplice** Partner in crime
*The **accomplice** of the smuggler was seen last night near dock yard.*
**Accomplish** Achieve
The Indian commandos can **accomplish** any difficult mission with their bravery.

14 **Accident** Meet with danger
*There was **accident** of two ships in high sea.*
**Occident** Western
The people of **Occident** countries have different cultural values.

15 **Accuse** Blame
*Why do you **accuse** me for your failure?*
**Excuse** Serve as reason
Teacher will not listen to any **excuses** of not doing home work.

16 **Acetic** Like vinegar
*Do you like **acetic** taste in salad?*
**Ascetic** Severely abstinent
The **ascetic** lives in a cave in the forest.

17 **Acme** Highest point
*Ramlalji is at **acme** of his business career.*
**Acne** Skin with pimples
**Acne** occurs due to various reasons but can be treated and prevented.

18 **Acquisitive** Keen to get things
*The curator should have an **acquisitive** nature.*
**Inquisitive** Curious
I have learnt a lot about science because of my **inquisitive** nature.

19 **Acute** Severe
*There is an **acute** cold in the polar regions.*
**Cute** Sweet looking
Little baby looks very **cute**.

20 **Ad** Short form of advertisement
*He is preparing an **ad** for his new product.*
**Add** Join, supplement
If you **add** two to three, the answer is five.
**Aid** Help
The army rushed to the **aid** of earthquake victims.

21 **Adapt** Adjust
*We can **adapt** ourselves to any condition if we want.*
**Adept** Expert
My brother is an **adept** in computer hardware.
**Adopt** Legally take a person into relationship
The childless couple **adopted** a baby from the orphanage.

22 **Addition** To add
*I want to add more points in my essay.*
**Edition** Published form of book
I am reading the last **edition** of "Formation of Words".

23 **Addict** Strong habit
He is a drug **addict**.
**Edict** Order of government
The new **edicts** are hard and fast.

24 **Adjudicate** Act as judge
*Will you **adjudicate** in our controversy?*
**Educate** Impart knowledge
It is very necessary to **educate** women and children in our country.

25 **Admission** Acceptance
*Will you give me **admission** in your college?*
**Admittance** Allow
Visitors are given **admittance** in the collector's office after prior permission.

26 **Adore** Love intensely
*I **adore** my wife.*
**Adorn** Decorate
Shahjahan **adorned** his palace with pearls and rubies.

27 **Adverse** Unfavourable
*Indian soldiers have to guard the borders in **adverse** conditions.*
**Averse** Dislike
She has strong **averse** to perfume smell.

28 **Advocaat** Liquor of eggs
*Have you tasted **advocaat**?*
**Advocate** Lawyer
My father is an **advocate** by profession.

29 **Aegis** Protection
*The cash was delivered under the **aegis** of private security.*
**Ages** Time
**Ages** ago dinosaurs walked on earth.

30 **Afar** At a distance
*Please, stand **afar** from the generator.*
**Affair** Matter
The Prime Minister will himself look in to **affairs** of defence.

31 **Affect** To influence
*This medicine will **affect** his fever.*
**Effect** Result
My advice has no **effect** on him.

32 **Afflict** To trouble
*Most of the persons of this locality are **afflicted** from breathing trouble.*
**Inflict** To lay on
In the battle Alexander **inflicted** crushing defeat on his enemies.

33 **Affection** Feeling of love
*All parents have deep **affection** for their children.*
**Affectation** False display
His behaviour is full of **affectation**.

34 **Affluent** Wealthy
*The farmer became **affluent** by hard work.*
**Effluent** Sewage of industries
**Effluent** of many industries is polluting the rivers.

35 **Afford** Have enough money for
*I cannot **afford** a luxurious car.*
**Effort** Attempts
His **efforts** will yield good results.

36 **Ago** Before particular time
*I had gone to London ten years **ago**.*
**Agog** Eager
He has a very **agog** child.

37 **Ail** To trouble
*Please don't **ail** me anymore.*
**Ale** Wine
Would you take some **ale** with dinner?

38 **Alms** Donation
*We give **alms** to the poor during good occasions.*
**Arms** Hands
The boxer has developed strong **arms**.

39 **Airy** Full of air
*We should live in an **airy** house.*
**Awry** Wrong
My boss has an **awry** notion about me.
**Hairy** Full with hair
Chimpanzee is a very **hairy** animal.

40 **Air** Atmosphere
*The **air** on the hills is refreshing.*
**Heir** One who inherits
Raj was declared an **heir** to the million dollar property.

41 **Alas** Express sorrow
*Alas!! That I had a long life.*
**Alias** Assumed name
Ramu **alias** Ramanlal is a runaway prisoner.

42 **Albumen** Egg-white
*John is cutting the **albumen** for cooking it.*
**Albumin** Water soluble protein
The doctor advised me to take **albumin** with water every day after dinner.

43 **Alder** Tree related to birch
*When did you plant **alder** in your garden?*
**Elder** More in age
My **elder** brother works in government office.

44 **Alight** Descend
*The pilot* ***alighted*** *from his plane.*
**Elite** Best group
The **elite** of the society should take more responsibility.

45 **Allay** Diminish
*The government is trying to* ***allay*** *the poverty ratio.*
**Alley** Narrow street
The balloon hawker passes through our **alley** every day.
**Ally** One who co-operates
Mr. Ram is business **allies**.

46 **Alleviate** Make less severe
*Can you help me* ***alleviate*** *my burden?*
**Elevate** Raise
The new pilot **elevates** the aircraft smoothly.

47 **All ready** All persons/things are ready
*Students are* ***all ready*** *for the test.*
**Already** At the moment
He has **already** left for the airport.

48 **All together** In a body
*Let us visit the minister* ***all together****.*
**Altogether** Completely
It is **altogether** impossible to do such a work.

49 **Allude** Refer to
*The English teacher often* ***alludes*** *to language of Churchill.*
**Elude** Escape
The criminal could not **elude** from the grasp of police.

50 **Allusion** Reference
*The professor gave an* ***allusion*** *of the creative genius of Shakespeare in the lecture.*
**Illusion** Deception
He has a self-**illusion** of being great.

51 **Altar** Place for worship or sacrifice
*The tribal leader arranged the ceremony at the **altar**.*
**Alter** Change
The engineer **altered** the original part with a duplicate part.

52 **Alteration** Change
*The project plan needs **alteration**.*
**Altercation** Dispute
There was some **altercation** between the two neighbours.

53 **Alumina** Aluminium oxide
*We use great quantity of **alumina** as raw material in our factory.*
**Alumnae** Former pupil
Jawaharlal Nehru was an **alumna** of Cambridge University.

54 **Amber** Yellow translucent fossilized resin used in jewellery
*The goldsmith is working with **ambers**.*
**Ember** Small piece of glowing coal
Many **embers** were seen in air when the wood was burnt.

55 **Amen** End of prayer, so be it
*The crowd shouted '**Amen**' at the end of prayer.*
**Omen** Prophetic significance
Many people believe in good and bad **omens**.

56 **Amiable** Likeable
*Everybody likes **amiable** person.*
**Amicable** Friendly
The two companies did not come to an **amicable** settlement.

57 **Anchor** Stabilizing thing
*The captain ordered to let go the **anchor** on the port.*
**Encore** Once more
The audience wishes the singer to **encore** the last song.

58 **Anchorage** Place for anchoring
*The sailors are planting the anchor on the **anchorage**.*
**Encourage** Give confidence
Parents should **encourage** their children to become good citizens.

59 **And** Also, in addition to
*Rahul **and** Mehul are twins.*
**End** Extreme limit
The **end** of this film was thrilling.

60 **Angel** Fairy, God's messenger
*Abu was an **angel**.*
**Angle** Corner
Make an **angle** of 90° in your notebook.
**Angle** Hook
The fisherman catches the fish with an **angle** from the pond.

61 **Animal** A living being
*Elephant is a very big **animal**.*
**Enamel** Glass like material for coating
The **enamel** in this colour is shining.

62 **Ant** Small insect
***Ant** likes sugar.*
**Ante** In front
The servant is cleaning the **ante** chamber.
**Aunt** A female relative
My **aunt** is coming tomorrow with my uncle.

63 **Anterior** Near the front
*People sitting at **anterior** can see the complete expressions of the actor.*
**Interior** Inner
We like beautiful and comfortable **interior** of a house.

64 **Antic** Tricks
*The lawyer's **antics** did not work in front of the judge.*
**Antique** Ancient piece of art
Numerous **antiques** are smuggled to other countries.

65 **Annual** Yearly
*The **annual** report was published.*
**Annul** Cancel
Please **annul** my name from the list of participants.

66 **Anvil** Tool of a shoe maker
*The cobbler is hammering constantly on his **anvil**.*
**Envy** Jealousy
Why do foreigners **envy** the progress of India?

67 **Apish** Like an ape
*The **apish** behaviour of these children will not create a good impression.*
**Uppish** Little up
The batsman could not play the **uppish** delivery.

68 **Appal** Horrifying
*We escaped from that **appalling** place with much difficulty.*
**Appeal** Plead
I **appealed** in Supreme Court for my case.
**Apple** One fruit
An **apple** a day keeps doctor away.

69 **Apposite** Proper
*The teacher made some **apposite** remarks for self-discipline.*
**Opposite** Contrary
He was **opposite** our party in election.

70 **Application** Request in writing

*I forwarded my **application** for promotion to the general manager.*

**Implication** Hidden meaning

We do not know the **implication** of China-Pakistan friendship.

71 **Arc** Part circumference of a circle

*Teacher asked him to draw a line crossing the **arc** of circle.*

**Arch** Curved structure of an opening, chief

The arch of this temple is very beautiful. England and Australia are **arch** rivals in cricket.

72 **Area** Region

*Rajasthan is the state with the largest **area** in India.*

**Aria** Long solo song

I was listening to an **aria** on the radio.

73 **Argent** Silvery white tincture

*How **argent** the moon looks in the black sky!*

**Urgent** Requiring immediate attendance

The doctor is **urgently** needed in the casualty ward.

74 **Aries** A zodiac sign

*His son was born under **Aries** sign.*

**Arris** Sharp edge

The **arris** of the sword should be good.

75 **Arrack** Alcoholic spirit

*There are many **arrack** shops in Rampur village.*

**Barrack** Living place for soldiers

The **barracks** are regularly cleaned by soldiers.

76 **Artificial** Not natural
*These are **artificial** flowers.*
**Artful** Cunning
The thief made an **artful** plan to escape.

77 **Artist** One who practices fine arts
*Sonu Nigam is a famous **artist**.*
**Artiste** Performer of dance song
The famous French **artiste** came to India for the big show.
**Artisan** Handicraft worker
Shahjahan had invited **artisans** from all over India.

78 **As** Appearing to be
*Building such **as** Taj Mahal is great tourist attraction.*
**Ass** Donkey
The potter over works his **ass**.

79 **Ash tray** Utensil to throw ash
*There is a golden **ash tray** on my table.*
**Astray** Out of the right way
The horse ran **astray** before the race.

80 **Aspire** Wish
*Who does not **aspire** to be wealthy?*
**Inspire** Encourage
Gandhiji **inspired** thousands of Indians to fight for freedom.

81 **Assay** Attempt something difficult
*Only if you assay in your work, it seems challenging.*
**Essay** Competition
Many students participated in **essay** competition.

82 **Assemble** Collect, gather
*The people **assembled** outside the hall to see the film star.*
**Ensemble** General effect
The **ensemble** of communal riots was widespread.

83 **Assign** Allot

*Sardar Patel was **assigned** the task to unite independent states of India.*

**Ensign** Banner, flag

Peace was declared as the white **ensign** was raised.

84 **Assure** Guarantee

*The sales officer **assured** me for replacement of the defective* piece.

**Azure** Sky-blue colour

The **azure** shirt looks good on you.

85 **Assume** Take to be true

*How can you **assume** that we would betray you?*

**Exhume** Dig up

Please **exhume** the ground quickly.

86 **Astern** Rear of ship/plane

*The bird dashed with the **astern** of a fighter plane.*

**Eastern** Related to east

The **eastern** part of India is covered by forest.

87 **At** Showing position

*The film will start **at** 9:00.*

**Ate** Past of eat

The monkey **ate** a banana from the child's hand.

88 **Attach** Affix

*Please **attach** a copy of your marksheet with this form.*

**Attaché** Specialist member of ambassador's staff

The **attached** of Pakistan was arrested for illegal activities.

89 **Audit** To check accounts
*I **audit** my business accounts regularly.*

90 **Auditor** One who checks accounts
*The **auditor** pointed out some mistakes in the accounts book.*
**Editor** Person who directs writing or films
The **Editor** of the *Times of India* writes a column every week.

91 **Aught** Anything
*I don't care **aught** for his order.*
**Ought** Must
We **ought** to serve our country.

92 **Aural** Of ear
*He is suffering from **aural** disease.*
**Oral** Not written, spoken
You must improve your **oral** communication.

93 **Auspicious** Good omen
*We celebrate the **auspicious** occasion of marriage with music colours.*
**Auspices** Patronage
Small kingdoms of India were united under the **auspices** of Sardar Patel.

94 **Aver** Assert
*The lawyer described many points to **aver** his case.*
**Ever** At all times
Have you **ever** felt as the king of the world?

95 **Avoid** Refrain
*We should **avoid** bad habits.*
**Ovoid** Eggs shaped
The little boy made an **ovoid** box.

96 **Avocation** Hobby
*Your **avocation** helps you to relax.*
**Vocation** Profession
My father is an architect by **vocation**.

97 **Award** Something that is granted
*I received the **award** of the best N.C.C. Cadet.*
**Reward** Return
I will give you a **reward** if you solve my problem.

98 **Awe** Reverential fear or wonder
*The messenger stood with **awe** in front of the emperor.*
**Owe** Debtor
I **owe** you some money.

99 **Awl** Small tool for piercing hole
*The tailor can use my **awl** for a week.*
**Awol** Absent without leave
Our servant has a bad habit of remaining on **awol** often.
**Owl** A nocturnal bird
Have you seen the big **owl** in the zoo?

100 **Axle** Spindle on which wheel turns
*The miller is working on the **axle** of his mill.*
**Excel** Surpass
She **excels** everybody in sports.

❑

# B

1 **Back** Behind
*Please don't stand **back** there.*
**Bake** Heat and cook
Can't you **bake** the bread properly?
**Beck** Brook
The rabbit bathed in the **beck**.

2 **Bacon** Meat of pig
*The butcher sells fresh **bacon** in his shop.*
**Beacon** Fire or light for warning
The captain ordered to shoot the **beacons** near the island.
**Beckon** Summon by gestures
The boss **beckoned** the engineer to enter the office.

3 **Bad** Ill
*He has controlled his **bad** temper.*
**Bade** Make an offer
He has **bade** me to start business with him.
**Bed** Place to sleep on
My **bed** is very comfortable to sleep.

4 **Badge** Emblem worn
*The regiment of a soldier can be known from his **badge**.*
**Budge** Move slightly
The car is stuck in mud its wheel doesn't **budge** at all.

5 **Bag** Container
*What is in your **big** bag?*
**Beg** To ask for
The old man **begs** in the market area for food and money.

6 **Bail** Security
*The police has asked for a **bail** of ₹ 50,000 to let go the prisoner.*
**Bale** A bundle
Many cotton **bales** are sold in market.
**Bell** Instrument creating sound
The peon rings the school **bell** at regular intervals.

7 **Bait** Food set to trap
*The fisherman puts small insects as **bait** for fish.*
**Bat** Play with bat
Sir Don Bradman **batted** well every time.
**Bet** Challenge
I don't like to **bet** for money.

8 **Bald** Hairless
*Ramukaka has become **bald** because of age.*
**Bold** Brave
Bhagat Singh was a very **bold** man.

9 **Balk** Hinder
*Why do you **balk** my work?*
**Bulk** Stock, quantity
If we like this item, we would buy it in **bulk**.

10 **Ball** A round toy
*Children are playing with a big **ball**.*
**Boll** Seed-vessel of cotton
The ladies are removing cotton from **boll**.

11 **Ballad** Slow sentimental poem

*There are many famous **ballads** in English.*

**Bollard** Short post on road

The cyclist dashed with the **bollard** and fell down.

12 **Ballet** A type of dance

*Have you seen the French **ballet**?*

**Ballot** Voting paper

We should teach the new voters, how to sign on **ballot** paper.

**Bullet** Thing which is shot from the gun

Each soldier was given twenty **bullets** to practice target.

13 **Balmy** Fragrant

*Whose **balmy** handkerchief is this?*

**Barmy** Stupid

I don't like to deal with such a **barmy** person.

**Barney** Noisy quarrel

There was a **barney** among the boys in the hostel.

14 **Ban** Not allow

*Government has put **ban** on many books.*

**Bun** Small round bread

Taste this **bun** with jam.

15 **Ban** Banish

*Anti-social element face **ban** from everywhere.*

**Bane** Ruin

The **bane** caused by the earthquake was terrible.

16 **Band** Group

*Robin Hood and his **band** helped the poor.*

**Bend** Force in to curve

Please don't **bend** this cover.

17 **Bang** Hit, throw

*The little boy **banged** the ball on the glass.*

**Bung** Stopper of cask

The thief broke the **bung** and stole away the things.

18 **Bangle** Ornament of hand

*Ladies are fond of gold **bangles**.*

**Bungle** Mismanage

Why does he **bungle** in his business?

19 **Banquet** Feast dinner

*Father has arranged a **banquet** to celebrate my return from UK.*

**Banquette** Upholstered bench

A wooden **banquette** was placed in the park for people.

20 **Bar** Place for alcoholic drinks

*The **bars** in our city close at 11.00 p.m.*

**Bar** Horizontal rod

Please put this **bar** inside the workshop.

21 **Barbel** Fresh water fish

*The fishermen of this village sell **barbel** to town people.*

**Barbell** Use for weightlifting

We have dozen **barbells** in our gymnasium.

22 **Bare** Naked

*Can you walk in desert with **bare** feet?*

**Bear** To tolerate, a wild animal

It is difficult to **bear** tooth ache. I saw a big grizzly **bear** in the zoo.

**Beer** Mild alcoholic drink

Don't drink too much **beer**, it increases fat.

23 **Barely** Just

***Barely** had he entered the office, when the bell rang.*

**Barley** Grain from which beer is made

They have a big cultivation of **barley**.

24 **Barrier** Partition

*There is Himalaya as a **barrier** between India and China.*

**Bearer** One who tolerates

Why should I be the **bearer** of his injustice?

25 **Barrow** Two-wheeled hand cart

*The horse has become weak to pull this **barrow**.*

**Borrow** To take as loan

Let us **borrow** money from the bank for our business.

**Burrow** Hole of rabbit

I saw a rabbit jumping into the **burrow**.

26 **Base** Foundation

*The **base** of our education should be strong.*

**Bash** Strike heavily

Why do you **bash** the poor horse like this?

**Bass** Lowest singing voice

Please adjust the **bass** in your song.

27 **Bask** Sun bath

*Europeans like to **bask** during spring.*

**Basque** Member of a people of the western Pyrenees

We met a **basque** there.

28 **Baste** Sew with large loose stitches

*The tailor was ordered to **baste** the tent of army.*

**Best** Excellent

Taj Mahal is the **best** monument in the world.

29 **Batter** Strike repeatedly
*The carpenter **battered** the design in the wooden block.*
**Better** More good
Shakespeare was a **better** writer than Johnson.

30 **Batsman** Who plays with bat
*Gavaskar was a great **batsman**.*
**Best Man** Excellent man
Raj is the **best man** in his family.

31 **Bawl** Speak loudly
*Why do you **bawl** sitting beside me?*
**Bowl** A vessel
Give me some milk in this **bowl**.

32 **Be** To become
*Ram will **be** an engineer.*
**Bee** An insect
Stay away or the **bee** will sting.

33 **Beach** Seashore
*Goa is famous for **beaches**.*
**Beech** Kind of tree
There are many **beech** trees in the public park.
**Bitch** Female dog
Our pet **bitch** gave birth to three sweet puppies.

34 **Bead** Small round piece
*Children can learn counting with **beads**.*
**Bid** Make an offer
He **bids** me to join his work.
**Bide** Wait for an opportunity
The soldiers will **bide** for attack sitting in the cave.

35 **Beaker** Vessel of laboratory
*The chemist is mixing chemicals in a **beaker**.*
**Bicker** Argue pettily
Don't **bicker** with them on such matters.

36 **Bean** Edible seeds
*Do you like the taste of **bean**?*
**Been** Visited, experienced
Have you **been** to London?
**Bin** Receptacle for rubbish
Throw these pieces of paper in the **bin**.

37 **Beat** Thrash
*You should not **beat** your horse so cruelly.*
**Beet** A vegetable
**Beet** is good to increase haemoglobin.
**Bit** Little, piece
There are some **bits** of bread for your parrot.

38 **Beautify** To make beautiful
*We will **beautify** our house before Diwali.*
**Beatify** Make happy
I would like to **beatify** children with these toys.

39 **Befall** Happen
*If you don't take care, accident will **befall**.*
**Befool** To cheat
Why does he **befool** his friends?

40 **Belay** Wind round a peg
*Please **belay** this string over there.*
**Delay** Get late
Don't **delay** in answering my question.

41 **Belch** Emit wind noisily through mouth
*The old Brahmin **belched** after having a heavy lunch.*
**Blench** Finch
The tiger's eyes **blenched** when the light fell on him.

42 **Belly** Stomach
*The doctor told me to control my **belly**.*
**Bally** Mild form of bloody
A **bally** war was fought between the two armies.
**Billy** Male goat
An old **billy** was brought in the zoo.

43 **Bell** Instrument creating sound
*There is a huge **bell** in the Church.*
**Belle** Beautiful woman
Helen of Troy was a famous legendary **belle**.

44 **Bellow** Sound of buffalo
*The buffalo **bellowed** on seeing its master.*
**Below** Down
Some monkeys are sitting **below** the tree.

45 **Berry** A fruit
***Berry** is my favourite fruit.*
**Bury** Forget, dig and lay in
Let us **bury** our differences.

46 **Berth** Seat in train or ship
*Please reserve the lower **berth** in the train.*
**Birth** Being born
What is your date of **birth**?

47 **Beside** By the side of
*I sit **beside** my friend in classroom.*
**Besides** Apart from
**Besides** one bungalow, I have two flats.

48 **Billion** Thousand million
*Earning a **billion** is very difficult.*
**Bullion** Silver-gold market
The **bullion** market is better for investment than share market.

49 **Bite** Cut with teeth
*Don't tease the cat, it will **bite** you.*
**Byte** Computing group
How many kilo-**bytes** are in your disk?

50 **Bitter** Pungent taste
*Nobody likes **bitter** food.*
**Beater** Instrument for beating
The shepherd uses whip as a **beater**.

51 **Blade** Cutting part
*I shave with a steel **blade**.*
**Bled** Past tense of bleed
His hand **bled** after injury.

52 **Bland** Taste less
*Please add some spices in this **bland** vegetable.*
**Blend** Mix
The cook **blends** flour with other things to prepare a tasty dish.

53 **Bleak** Exposed
*Keep your cut **bleak**.*
**Blink** Closing and opening of eyes
Fish cannot **blink**.

54 **Bless** Bestow good wishes
*Let God **bless** us for our good work.*
**Bliss** Happiness and peace
The tourists find **bliss** in the nature of Himalayas.

55 **Blew** Past of blow

*The wind **blew** with noise at the seashore.*

**Blue** A colour

Our school uniform is **blue** trousers and white shirt.

**Blues** Bout of depression

Doctor advised the patient to visit a lovely place to recover from his **blues**.

56 **Bloat** Inflate

*He is **bloated** by his sudden success.*

**Blot** Spot-stain

The **blot** of oil cannot be removed easily.

57 **Bloc** Group sharing common purpose

*We have formed a **bloc** for social work.*

**Block** Solid piece of wood-stone

The sculptor will carve an idol from this **block**.

**Bloke** Fellow

What is that **bloke** doing in darkness?

58 **Blush** Feel shy

*The bride **blushed** on seeing her husband.*

**Bluish** Slightly blue

Do you like the **bluish** shade in this room?

59 **Boar** Pig

*Be away from that wild **boar**.*

**Bore** To trouble

I am **bored** of staying alone.

60 **Boat** Canoe

*Fisherman's only vehicle is a **boat**.*

**Bought** Past of buy

I **bought** some toys for children.

61 **Bogie** Wheeled carriage of locomotive
*There are hundred people travelling in this* ***bogie****.*
**Bogey** Score of Golf
John works in a club; he keeps the **bogey** during tournament.

62 **Bollocks** Nonsense
*Why did he write* ***bollocks*** *in his letter?*
**Bullocks** Oxen
That is a fine pair of **bullocks**.

63 **Bon** Sweet
*Children like the* ***bon*** *taste of chocolates.*
**Bone** Part of skeleton
There are many **bones** in a human body.

64 **Bond** Thing or force that unites
*There should be strong* ***bond*** *of relation between husband and wife.*
**Bound** Limitations
Before the army could reach the criminals went out of **bound**.

65 **Bonny** Attractive physically
*The* ***bonny*** *models have large demand.*
**Bony** Thin with bones
Though he is **bony**, he is very strong.

66 **Boom** Economic prosperity
*There was a great* ***boom*** *in U.S.A. after the industrial revolution.*
**Boon** Blessing
Arjun asked Lord Krishna for a **boon**.

67 **Bootee** Baby's soft shoes
*Do you like that soft-pink* ***bootee****?*
**Booty** Loot
There was a quarrel among bandits for the share of the **booty**.

68 **Booth** Place for voting
*There is a long queue at the* ***booth****.*
**Both** Involving two persons
**Both** Sita and Gita are selected in the team.

69 **Born** Come into existence
*Gandhiji was* ***born*** *on 2nd October, 1869.*
**Borne** To tolerate
We had **borne** such an intensive pain.

70 **Bosh** Nonsense
*Don't talk* ***bosh*** *with me.*
**Boss** Employer
My **boss** gave me much accounting work.

71 **Boy** Male child
*Kishan is a handsome* ***boy****.*
**Buoy** Anchored float as mask
The swimming race was to reach the **buoy** and come back.

72 **Brad** Thin flat nail
*I will hang the picture on that* ***brad****.*
**Bread** An eatable
Sandwich is made from **bread**.
**Bred** Raise
Ami seems a well-**bred** girl.

73 **Brake** Used to stop vehicle
*Fast vehicles should have strong* ***brakes****.*
**Break** Cut
The glass **breaks** easily.

74 **Branch** Bough
*The banyan tree has strong* ***branches****.*
**Brunch** Combine breakfast and lunch
I start my work after having **brunch**.

75 **Brash** Self-assertive
*Do you like if I become **brash**?*
**Brush** Implement with bristles
We clean our teeth with a soft **brush**.

76 **Brawn** Muscular strength
*The Gorilla showed his **brawn** when teased.*
**Brown** Colour of wood
I like your **brown** T-shirt.

77 **Break out** Spread
*Malaria **breaks out** in our city every year.*
**Outbreak** Break out hostilities
The **outbreak** of Indian soldiers against British in 1857 is a well-known event.

78 **Bridal** Related to marriage
*From where did you buy your beautiful **bridal** dress?*
**Bridle** Control
A good trainer knows how to keep the horse under **bridle**.

79 **Broach** Raise for discussion
*I will **broach** the financial matter in the board's meeting.*
**Brooch** Ornamental pin
Is your **brooch** studded with diamonds?

80 **Bruit** Spread
*The disease was **bruit** in the entire city.*
**Brute** Unpleasant person
I stay away from **brutes**.

81 **Brunt** Impact of an attack
*I had a severe **brunt** of malaria.*
**Burnt** Which is burn
Tommy likes **burnt** breads.

82 **Budge** Move slightly
*I did not **budge** till my programme was over.*
**Buzz** Hum of bee
The bees **buzz** around the hive.

83 **Bun** Small round bread
*Do you like **bun** and cheese?*
**Burn** On fire, ignite
We **burn** wood for warmth in winter.

84 **Burst** Break violently
*We **burst** balloons in birthday party.*
**Bust** Sculpture till human chest
The **bust** of Tagore is placed in our hall.

85 **Buster** Fellow
*Who was that **buster** sitting on my car?*
**Duster** To wipe writings
Teacher rubbed the sum with the **duster**.

86 **But** However
*I would like to come **but** I am sick.*
**Butt** Thicker end of a gun
The soldier kept the **butt** on his shoulder to aim.

87 **Buy** To get something on paying
*We **buy** fruits from market every day.*
**By** Near
Sit **by** me to talk.
**Bye** Fare well
'Good **bye**' said the boy to his friends.

❑

# C

1 **Cabal** Intrigue
*Who could have planned such a cunning* ***cabal****?*
**Cable** Wire
This is an Internet **cable**.

2 **Cache** Hiding place of treasure
*The pirates had kept a big cave as* ***cache****.*
**Catch** To hold
**Catch** this ball quickly.

3 **Calendar** Chart showing dates
*This new* ***calendar*** *is for 2012.*
**Calender** Press cloth
**Calender** my coat.

4 **Call** To summon
***Call*** *the boys in to the class.*
**Caul** Membrane enclosing a foetus
The doctor is treating the lady for **caul**.

5 **Called** To summon
*I have* ***called*** *all my friends for my birthday party.*
**Cold** Very cool
This winter was very **cold**.

6 **Callous** Insensitive
*Her husband is a very **callous** person.*
**Callus** Area of hard thick skin
The doctor cut off the **callus** from my sole.

7 **Campion** Wild plant
*We find many **campions** near the river bank.*
**Champion** Who wins everywhere
The people surrounded the **champion**.

8 **Can** Capable
*I **can** fly a plane.*
**Cane** Stem of plant
The horse trainer keeps a **cane** to threaten it.

9 **Canal** Outlet for water
*The **canal** from the dam supplies us water.*
**Channel** Course in which thing moves
Gandhiji **channelized** people for freedom movement.

10 **Cannon** Big sun
*The sudden roar of the **cannons** frightened us.*
**Canon** Rule
We should not violate **canon** of traffic.

11 **Canvas** A kind of rough cloth
*His shoes are made of **canvas**.*
**Canvass** Ask for votes
I am **canvassing** for my own candidate.

12 **Cap** Type of hat
*People wear **cap** for protection against sun.*
**Cape** Head land, sleeveless coat
**Cape** of Good Hope is a famous place.

13 **Capital** — Chief city
*New Delhi is the* ***capital*** *of India.*
**Capitol** — Name given to important public building
Many people gathered at the **capitol** today.

14 **Captain** — One who leads
*An able* ***captain*** *can lead the team to victory.*
**Caption** — Wording appended
The company has put a **caption** in its signboard.

15 **Card** — A thick paper used in game or sending message
*Thanks for your birthday* ***card****.*
**Curd** — Thick butter milk
Take this spoon to eat **curd**.

16 **Career** — Life-profession
*You must work for your* ***career****.*
**Carrier** — Those who carry
The **carriers** went on strike.

17 **Cares** — To keep watch
*Mother* ***cares*** *for her children.*
**Caress** — To fondle
Parents like to **caress** their children.

18 **Carnal** — Of the flesh
*We should not care only for* ***carnal*** *pleasures in life.*
**Kernel** — Essence of anything
What is the **kernel** of the *Gita*?

19 **Carpal** — Wrist bone
*The sportsman had an injury on the* ***carpal****.*
**Carpel** — Reproductive organ of plant
The scientist is dissecting a **carpel** for research.

20 **Carton** Box for packing
*I found ten **cartons** of tea in his shop.*
**Cartoon** Comic characters
Children as well as elders like **cartoons**.

21 **Carve** Engrave
*Taj Mahal is **carved** from marble.*
**Crave** To long for
The old woman **craved** to see her son.

22 **Case** Matter, situation
*The new lawyer is studying some **cases**.*
**Cash** Hard money
I have got some **cash** in my pocket.

23 **Casemate** Armoured enclosure
*The army has prepared a **casemate** near border.*
**Casement** Window
Do not throw out paper from the **casement**, throw it into the dustbin.

24 **Cast** Throw
***Cast** off your old cloths.*
**Caste** Community
He is a Rajput by **caste**.

25 **Casual** Occasional
*He is on his **casual** visit to the club.*
**Causal** Related to cause
Carelessness was the **causal** of this accident.

26 **Cater** Supply food
*The waiters will **cater** as per your order.*
**Crater** Mouth of volcano
We should stay away from **craters**.

27 **Cation** Positively charged

*The wire has **cation**.*

**Caution** Warning

There is a **caution** on the electric pole.

28 **Cattle** Group of animals

*The **cattle** graze in pastures in the morning.*

**Kettle** Vessel for storing tea

There is no coffee in this **kettle**.

29 **Caw** Cry of crow or cock

*The cock **caws** at morning.*

**Cow** An animal

Have you seen that big white **cow**?

30 **Cease** Stop

*When will this rain **cease**?*

**Siege** Surround

Akbar's army laid a **siege** to the Fort of Udaipur.

**Seize** To catch

**Seize** the opportunity when it comes.

31 **Celibate** One who doesn't marry

*Why has he decided to remain a **celibate**?*

**Celebrate** To enjoy on particular occasion

In India, people **celebrate** many festivals with family and friends.

32 **Celery** A plant used as a vegetable

*This **celery** tastes good.*

**Salary** Payment in return of work

My company pays me a good **salary**.

33 **Cell** Underground room
*Cash is kept in the **cell** in this bank.*
**Sale** To put up sell
What did you buy from the crockery **sale**?
**Sell** To give in exchange of money
The hawkers **sell** fruits in market.

34 **Cello** A bass instrument of violin family
*He is an artist of **cello**.*
**Shallow** Not deep
Children can enter in this **shallow** water.

35 **Cemetery** Funeral place
*There is broad land for **cemetery** behind the Church.*
**Symmetry** Harmony
The expert architect can take care of complete **symmetry** of building.

36 **Censer** Vessel for burning incense
*I am cleaning this **censer**.*
**Censor** Official licensing
The film has already been approved by the **censor**.
**Censure** To criticise
The people **censure** corrupt politicians.

37 **Cent** A currency
*How many **cents** do you have in your pocket?*
**Scent** Sweet smell
I like mild **scent**.

38 **Century** Hundred
*How many **centuries** has Sachin scored?*
**Sanctuary** Protected area for animals
The only lion **sanctuary** of Asia is in Gujarat.

39 **Cereal** Edibles
*The price of **cereals** has gone up.*
**Serial** Series of episodes
We can see many **serials** on television.

40 **Cession** An act of giving up
*Our government demands the **cession** of terrorism in Kashmir.*
**Session** Period of sitting
Parliament is in **session** these days.

41 **Chafe** Become sore
*Why does he get **chafe** by our jokes?*
**Chaff** Husks of corn, etc.
We burn **chaff** to drive away mosquitoes.
**Chef** Head cook
The **chef** of this hotel is an expert in soups.

42 **Chair** Used for sitting
*Is this **chair** comfortable?*
**Char** Make black by burning
He **charred** his wooden stick in fire.

43 **Chaise** Horse-drawn cart for two
*It is safer to travel in **chaise**.*
**Chase** Follow
Don't **chase** wild animals without weapon.

44 **Chalk** Pen of lime for writing
*You can use this **chalk** on the blackboard.*
**Choke** Not allowed to breathe
The atmosphere was **choking** because of the smoke.

45 **Chary** Cautious
*The management has to take a **chary** step.*
**Cherry** A sweet fruit
**Cherry** with ice-cream tastes good.

46 **Chase** Follow, go after
*Cat **chases** mouse.*
**Chess** An indoor game
**Chess** is a good exercise for mind.

47 **Chaste** Pure, virtuous
*We should have company of **chaste** people.*
**Chest** Upper part of body, big box
The bodybuilder has a broad **chest**.
There are some jewels in that **chest**.

48 **Cheap** Not costly
*The furniture is **cheap** but very good.*
**Chip** Piece
Here are some **chips** of apple for you.

49 **Cheat** To do wrong
*It is not good to **cheat** anybody.*
**Chit** Small piece of paper with message
I will write a **chit** for reference to the manager.

50 **Check** Examine, restrain
*Do not **check** him from going there.*
**Cheque** Order for money
I have issued a **cheque** in your name.

51 **Cheek** Part of face
*The little baby's **cheeks** are soft and red.*
**Chick** Young bird
The **chicks** are playing in the puddle.

52 **Chide** Scold
*Why did you **chide** him?*
**Child** An infant
That **child** is an orphan.

53 **Chilli** Hot
*My soup has **chilli** taste.*
**Chilly** Cold
**Chilly** wind was blowing yesterday.

54 **Choler** Anger
***Choler** is not good for your health.*
**Collar** Part of shirt
Please, iron the **collar** of my shirt properly.

55 **Choral** Sung by a chorus
*They sing **choral** very well.*
**Chorale** Simple hymn
He writes **chorales** for religious and social functions.

56 **Chord** String of musical instrument
***Chord** of my guitar broken.*
**Cord** String
Will you give me a fishing **cord**?

57 **Cite** To quote
*You can **cite** many examples from the Ramayana.*
**Site** Situation
That is the **site** for our new factory.
**Sight** Able to see, scene
Sun rise at sea shore is a beautiful **sight**.

58 **Civil** Of citizens
*He is a member of a **civil** body.*
**Civics** Study of rights and duties of citizens
Study of **civics** should be compulsory at college level and not at school level.

| | | |
|---|---|---|
| 59 | **Cliché** | Hackneyed phrase |
| | *Why do you use so many* ***clichés*** *in your articles?* | |
| | **Clinch** | Settle |
| | I will **clinch** this business for some years. | |
| 60 | **Climactic** | Event or point of greatest intensity or interest |
| | *The drama is at the* ***climactic*** *situation now.* | |
| | **Climatic** | Related to climate |
| | The **climatic** condition is getting better in India. | |
| 61 | **Cloak** | Rob |
| | *The kings used to wear silk* ***cloaks****.* | |
| | **Clock** | Instrument showing time |
| | Wind the **clock** and put it on the wall. | |
| 62 | **Clobber** | Beat |
| | *The police had to* ***clobber*** *the mob to disperse them.* | |
| | **Cobbler** | One who mends shoes |
| | That **cobbler** mends perfectly. | |
| 63 | **Cloth** | Material made by cotton, silk, etc. |
| | *He is a* ***cloth*** *merchant.* | |
| | **Clothe** | To wear cloth |
| | I will **clothe** properly for the party. | |
| 64 | **Cloud** | Opaque white patch in sky |
| | *The* ***clouds*** *are moving fast in sky.* | |
| | **Clout** | Heavy blow |
| | It was difficult for me to recover from **clout** in business. | |
| 65 | **Coal** | A mineral used for burning |
| | *We use* ***coal*** *as fuel in our factory.* | |
| | **Cole** | Cabbage |
| | **Cole** vegetable is prepared well in this restaurant. | |

66 **Coarse** Rough
*His behaviour is **coarse**.*
**Course** Line of action, syllabus
**Course** of engineering has changed this year.

67 **Coast** Shore
*The ship is nearing the **coast**.*
**Cost** Price
What is the **cost** of this car?

68 **Coat** A garment
*He is wearing a woollen **coat**.*
**Cot** Small bed
I will rest for a while on this **cot**.
**Cote** Shelter for birds, animals
The shepherd has put his ducks in the **cote**.
**Quote** To repeat someone's words
Our teacher could **quote** Shakespeare easily.

69 **Coax** To persuade
*How did he **coax** the customer to buy two items?*
**Cox** One who leads directs
Tony is a **cox** in a boat.

70 **Cockle** Edible shell fish
***Cockle** is our favourite food.*
**Cackle** Sound of goose
Can you hear **cackle** from the pond?

71 **Coco** Coconut
*Would you have some **coco** water with bread?*
**Cocoa** Powder from which chocolate is made
Don't put so much **cocoa** in the preparation of cake.

72 **Cod** A fish
*I saw the **cod** in an aquarium.*
**Code** Secret language
Captain talked with the soldiers in **code** language.

73 **Coif** Fitting cap
*I use **coif** in winter to protect myself from cold.*
**Coiff** Dress or arrange hair
She can **coiff** her hair elegantly.

74 **Collage** Make a thing by sticking
*Children can develop **collage** as a hobby.*
**College** Centre of higher studies
In which **college** do you study?

75 **Collagen** Protein found in animal tissue
*The scientist is working on **collagen**.*
**Collegian** One who studies in college
My son is now a **collegian**.

76 **Collide** Dash
*Our car **collided** with a truck.*
**Colloid** Substance with particles
Is this made of **colloid**?
**Collude** Conspire together
The members of the gang will **collude** for robbery.

77 **Cologne** Fragrant water
*Spray some **cologne** and feel fresh.*
**Colon** A punctuation mark
Do you know where to use **colon**?

78 **Coma** Unconscious state
*The patient recovered from **coma**.*
**Comma** A punctuation mark
Students of grammar should know when to use **comma**.

79 **Comity** Friendship
*Can there be **comity** between us?*
**Committee** A group formed to do some task.
The government has formed a **committee** to inquire about the scandal.

80 **Commend** Praise
*I should **commend** your admirable work.*
**Comment** To give one's views
Will you **comment** on this painting?

81 **Commiserate** Express sympathy
*By donating generously I **commiserate** towards the earth quake victims.*
**Commissariat** Department of government
My father is a senior officer in the **commissariat**.

82 **Cook** To prepare food
*Do you **cook** in oven?*
**Kook** Crazy person
Who will deal with that **kook**?

83 **Complement** Which completes
*Woman is a **complement** of man.*
**Compliment** Expression of praise
She was pleased with the **compliments** paid to her.

84 **Confidant** Trusted person
*Manmohan is my **confidant**.*
**Confident** Sure and certain
Are you **confident** of your success?

85 **Contagious** A disease which spreads by contact
*Smallpox is a **contagious** disease.*
**Contiguous** Near
The post office is **contiguous** to our office.

86 **Corporal** Physical

*We should not give **corporal** punishment to children.*

**Corporeal** With a body

Spirits are not **corporeal** beings.

87 **Corps** Division of army

*He has joined the National Cadet **Corps**.*

**Corpse** Dead body

My heart was moved on seeing a **corpse**.

88 **Council** Assembly

*He is a member of the Legislative **Council**.*

**Counsel** Advice

Why should he accept my **counsel**?

89 **Cue** Last words of actor before another enters

*He said the **cue** slowly.*

**Queue** Line

There is a big **queue** for reservation.

90 **Cymbal** A musical instrument

*I like the sweet music of **cymbal**.*

**Symbol** Sign

Navigators use many **symbols** in their work.

❑

# D

1 **Dad** Father
*I have a loving **dad**.*
**Dead** Not alive, died
The terrorists were shot **dead** by jawans.

2 **Dairy** Milk depot
*We visited a co-operative **dairy**.*
**Diary** A note book
Do you have a habit of writing a **diary**?

3 **Dam** Reservoir
*There was a lot of water in the **dam** before summer.*
**Dame** Girl
Look at that fashionable **dame**.
**Damn** Condemn
I **damn** the traitors of India.

4 **Damp** Little wet
*My shirt is **damp**.*
**Dump** Heap
We should not **dump** rubbish everywhere.

5 **Dance** Move in rhythm
*Let us **dance** on this music.*
**Dunce** Dullard
Your brother is a **dunce**.

6 **Dane** Type of dog
*The Duke use his **dane** for hunting.*
**Den** Cave
Who would dare to go in the **den** of a lion?

7 **Date** Day of month
*What is your birth **date**?*
**Debt** Money owed
He is in my **debt** for ₹ 20,000/.

8 **Dawn** Early morning
*It is refreshing to walk at **dawn**.*
**Don** Boss of gangster
The police arrested the underworld **don**.
**Down** Below
Will you get **down** from the tree?

9 **Dean** Head
*I met the **dean** of our institution for research paper.*
**Din** Noise
What is this entire **din** for?

10 **Dear** Loved one
*My family members are **dear** to me.*
**Deer** Animal
**Deer** runs very fast.

11 **Debar** Stop
*The government can **debar** anyone caught doing wrong.*
**Debark** Get out of a boat
Many passengers **debarked** at the port of Goa.

12 **Debauch** Debase
*Vicious man **debauches** others.*
**Debouch** Come out
A sweet chick **debouched** from an egg.

13 **Decease** To die
*The old man's sudden **decease** was shock to the family.*
**Disease** Illness
What is the cure of this **disease**?

14 **Decent** Civilized
*The young man has **decent** manners.*
**Descent** Come down
The **descent** of the hill was very tough.
**Dissent** Differ
I sent a note of **dissent** to the President.

15 **Declension** Decline
*The **declension** of the Mogul Empire is an important part of Indian history.*
**Declination** Downward
There is **declination** trend in the share market.

16 **Decree** Order
*You have to respect the court's **decree**.*
**Decry** Be little
Many times honest people are **decried** by others.
**Degree** Unit of measurement
He has high **degree** of temperature.

17 **Debtor** Person owing money
*Is he your bank's **debtor**?*
**Deter** Stop
Why did you **deter** me in my work?
**Detour** Change course
The boat will **detour** from this point.

18 **Deed** Brave work
*Indian soldiers are famous for their **deeds**.*
**Did** Work done
He **did** his homework speedily.

19 **Deem** Judge
*You cannot **deem** anyone's intention from face.*
**Dim** Not bright
The evening is becoming **dim**.

20 **Deep** Far down
*Nothing is as **deep** as the ocean.*
**Dip** Immerse
**Dip** the toast in the soup.

21 **Defence** Protect
*We should have a powerful **defence** mechanism.*
**Defiance** Challenge
He lost everything in **defiance** on petty matter.

22 **Deference** Limitation
*We must show due **deference** to our elders.*
**Difference** Different
There is no **difference** between your style and mine.

23 **Defy** Challenge
*You will be penalized if you **defy** the ban imposed by the government.*
**Deify** Worship
Gandhiji is **deified** in the whole of the world.

24 **Delicate** Fragile
*Small children have **delicate** limbs.*
**Delinquent** Culprit
Who was proved the **delinquent** in the court?

25 **Delude** Cheat
*He can no longer be **deluded** by false promises.*
**Elude** Escape
He was so clever that he **eluded** police in no time.

26 **Demur** Oppose
*Why do your **demur** my point every time?*
**Demure** Modest
I appreciate his **demure** personality.

27 **Depose** Throw away from post
*The inspector was **deposed** after corruption charges.*
**Dispose** Exhaust
We will **dispose** the scrape in furnace.

28 **Deposition** Sworn evidence
*The witness was brought in court for **deposition**.*
**Disposition** Arrangement
Under whose **disposition** is this function held?

29 **Deprecate** Hate
*Pakistan **deprecates** our foreign policy.*
**Depreciate** Under value
The share price has **depreciated**.

30 **Depreciation** Wear and tear
*What is the **depreciation** value of this vehicle?*
**Depression** Extreme sadness
He is suffering from **depression** because of loss in business.

31 **Desert** Barren place
*We can see camels in a **desert**.*
**Deserts** Deserve
The murderer was hanged, so he got his **deserts**.
**Dessert** Sweet dish
The **dessert** course consisted of cake and ice-cream.

32 **Desperate** Trying very much
*The athlete made **desperate** try to win.*
**Disparate** Different
What is so **disparate** about these two brothers?

33 **Devastate** Ruin
*The cyclone **devastated** many villages.*
**Divest** Expose
We will **divest** your scandals.

34 **Device** Plan
*He used a strange **device** to deceive me.*
**Devise** To plan
The enemy **devised** many plans against us, but of no use.

35 **Devote** To give
*The merchant will **devote** his time for his old parents.*
**Devotee** Worshipper
Narsinh Mehta was a **devotee** of Lord Krishna.

36 **Dew** Water vapour
*Look at the **dew** drops on grass.*
**Due** Appropriate
Give me back my **due**.

37 **Die** Death
*The old men will **die** soon.*
**Dye** To colour
Will you **dye** my dress?

38 **Dinar** One currency
*How many **dinars** does he earn?*
**Diner** One who dines
All the **diners** are at the table.
**Dinner** Evening meal
We have invited some guests for **dinner**.

39 **Discreet** Modest
*It was a very **discreet** decision.*
**Discrete** Different
He is a very **discrete** person.

40 **Discus** Plate
*The players are playing with* ***discus****.*
**Discuss** Argue
The board will **discuss** important matters in this meeting.

41 **Distort** Ruin the shape
*The robbers* ***distorted*** *the safe.*
**Distraught** Sad
Why are you in a **distraught** mood today?

42 **Distrain** Seize
*Police can* ***distrain*** *upon any illegal goods.*
**Distrait** Inattentive
Why is your son so **distrait** in his studies?

43 **Divers** Person going under the sea
*Some* ***divers*** *can remain under water for hours.*
**Diverse** Varied
People have **diverse** opinion about the affair.

44 **Dole** Donation
*How much* ***dole*** *did the institution receive?*
**Doll** Toy
The girls like to play with **doll**.

45 **Dollar** Currency
*He has earned many* ***dollars*** *in U.S.A.*
**Dolour** Sadness
What is the cause of your **dolour**?

46 **Door** Barrier for closing room
*Please shut the* ***door****.*
**Dour** Stern
Don't be **dour** in your attitude.

47 **Dose** Portion of medicine

*He has taken four* ***doses*** *of mixture.*

**Doss** Place to sleep

The traveller paid much money for the **doss** in this new place.

**Doze** Nap

Let him sleep he is **dozing**.

48 **Dot** Small mark

*Put a* ***dot*** *on i.*

**Dote** Be fond of

He waits **dotingly** for his beloved.

49 **Draught** Portion of medicine drink

*She drank milk in one* ***draught****.*

**Drought** Dry weather

The **drought** caused famine in the state.

50 **Droop** Bend down

*The old lady* ***droops*** *due to age.*

**Drop** Let go

The fielder **dropped** the catch.

51 **Dual** Double

***Dual*** *policy is never good.*

**Duel** Fight between two

He died in a **duel**.

52 **Duck** A bird

***Duck*** *swims swiftly.*

**Duct** Pipe

The water **duct** is choked.

53 **Dully** Lazily

*Don't work **dully**.*

**Duly** Properly

The servant will be **duly** paid for his work.

54 **Done** Do work

*I have **done** some good job.*

**Dun** Grey colour

The smoke looks **dun**.

❑

# E

1 **Each** Everyone
***Each** player was given uniform.*
**Etch** Carve
Can the artisan **etch** idol from this piece of chalk?
**Itch** Sensation of skin
Apply this ointment where you feel an **itch**.

2 **Earn** Get money
*How much do you **earn** from your grocery business?*
**Urn** A utensil
Pour some milk into the **urn**.

3 **Earth** Our planet
***Earth** is the home of humans.*
**Hearth** Vessel for burning
Food is boiling on the **hearth**.

4 **East** One direction
*Sun rises in the **East**.*
**Yeast** Fermentation
Many food items are prepared from **yeast**.

5 **Eat** Chew
*Do you like to **eat** dark chocolate?*
**It** Used for non-living
**It** is a beautiful flower.

6 **Economic** Related to economics
*Let us discuss the* ***economic*** *aspect of the new policy.*
**Economics** Study of money
I studied **economics** in college.

7 **Egoism** Self-interest
*His* ***egoism*** *is not good.*
**Egotism** Self-conceit
Your **egotism** is harmful to you.

8 **Egoistical** Self-interested person
*His* ***egoistical*** *behaviour was not liked by anybody.*
**Egotistical** Self-conceited person
**Egotistical** person are unwelcomed everywhere.

9 **Eject** Take out
*You can* ***eject*** *the CD from the player.*
**Deject** Sadden
She was **dejected** by her college grade.

10 **Elicit** Draw from
*His speech* ***elicited*** *praise from one and all.*
**Illicit** Unlawful
He carries on an **illicit** trade in drugs.

11 **Eligible** Fit
*Is he* ***eligible*** *for this post?*
**Illegible** Unreadable
Your hand-writing is **illegible**.

12 **Elusive** Difficult to remember
*These chemical formulas are* ***elusive***.
**Illusive** False impression
Beware of his **illusive** personality.

13 **Embarrass** Feel shame

*I was **embarrassed** by my child's behaviour in the party.*

**Embrace** Hold in arms

The two friends **embraced** each other as they met after long time.

14 **Emerge** Come out

*He saw a tiger **emerging** out of the bushes.*

**Immerse** Plunge into

Don't **immerse** your hand into the boiling water.

15 **Emigrant** Person who leaves the country to settle in another country

*Many **emigrants** from Bangladesh have come to India.*

**Immigrant** Who comes to the other country

Mr. Patel is an aspiring **immigrant** to Canada.

16 **Eminent** Famous

*C.V. Raman was an **eminent** scientist.*

**Immanent** Omnipresent

God is **immanent**.

17 **Empire** Kingdom

*Ashoka had a vast **empire**.*

**Umpire** One who decides

**Umpire's** decision is always final.

18 **Empress** Queen

*Victoria was the **empress** of England.*

**Impress** To press, stamp, print

He can **impress** anybody by his personality.

19 **Empty** Nothing in
*The container is **empty**.*
**Impiety** Lack of piety
There is **impiety** in your attitude.
**Umpteen** Innumerable
He has asked this question **umpteen** times.

20 **Enable** Strengthen
*Please **enable** me to take up this noble cause.*
**Unable** Not able
Are you **unable** to convince them?

21 **Enjoin** Order
*What was the result of his **enjoin**?*
**Enjoy** Be happy
We will **enjoy** our party.

22 **Ensue** To happen after
*I could judge the incident that was to **ensue**.*
**Ensure** Secured
Good return is **ensured** by the insurance company.
**Insure** Take insurance
I have **insured** my life for a big amount.

23 **Entente** Agreement
*The terms of this **entente** are complex.*
**Intent** Engrossed
He was so **intent** in reading that he did not hear my voice.

24 **Envelop** To cover
*If we don't take care, pollution will **envelop** the earth.*
**Envelope** Wrapper
I sent the **envelope** by courier.

25 **Erotic** Pertaining to love
*Children should be kept away from **erotic** films and books.*
**Erratic** Uncertain
His **erratic** behaviour will hinder his progress.

26 **Estimate** Calculation
*What is your **estimate** about the new project?*
**Estimation** Opinion
He has gone down in our **estimation**.

27 **Eternal** Forever
*Sun shines **eternally**.*
**Internal** Inside
He had some **internal** injury.

28 **Evade** Avoid
*They are trying to **evade** competition with us.*
**Invade** Attack
No foreign army would dare to **invade** India.

29 **Evasion** Avoidance
*What is the reason of my **evasion**?*
**Invasion** Attack
How many times did the **invasion** take place?

30 **Evoke** Draw feelings
*The poet has tried to **evoke** for God in this song.*
**Invoke** Call on
They will **invoke** their relatives for function.

31 **Evolve** Unfold
*Many facts **evolved** from this case.*
**Involve** Include
Why don't you **involve** him in your mission?

32 **Exalt** Raise in rank
*Did your boss **exalt** you for your good work?*
**Exult** Extreme joy
I will **exult** after my success.

33 **Excerpt** Extract
*We saw some **excerpts** of the new film.*
**Expert** Skilful
Dr. Singh is an **expert** in astronomy.

34 **Excite** Provoke
*Don't **excite** those monkeys.*
**Exist** Alive
No man can **exist** without relations.
**Exit** Go out
He **exited** from the back door.

35 **Excrete** Throw out
*Scavengers eat **excreted** matter.*
**Execrate** Hate
Why does she **execrate** me?

36 **Excursion** Go on picnic
*We love **excursions** in the hills.*
**Incursion** Attack
What was the cause of **incursion** of malaria?

37 **Executioner** Who carries out death sentence
*An **executioner's** life is not a pleasant one.*
**Executor** One who executes will
Whom has your father nominated as his **executor**?

38 **Exhale** Breathe out
***Exhale** deeply for relaxation.*
**Exile** Banish
Lord Ram was sent to **exile** by his parents.

39 **Expand** Lengthen
*I am thinking to **expand** my business.*
**Expend** Spend
I will *expend* much to get what I want.

40 **Expansive** Extensive
*I am director of an **expansive** factory.*
**Expensive** Costly
This car is very **expensive**.

41 **Expatiate** Speak at length
*Would you **expatiate** on your recent tour to Europe?*
**Expatriate** Banish
The government has decided to **expatriate** all communal criminals.
**Extirpate** Destroy
We can **extirpate** wastage with this technology.

42 **Explicit** Clearly
*There is **explicit** instruction on the paper.*
**Implicit** Perfect
This is an **implicit** proof.

43 **Extant** Existing
*Some bad conditions are **extant** in our country.*
**Extent** Degree
The **extent** of damage caused by flood is not known yet.

44 **Extinct** Destroyed
*Dinosaurs are **extinct** now.*
**Instinct** Inborn impulse
Animals have more powerful **instinct** than humans.

45 **Eyes** Organ of sight
***Eyes** are extremely precious.*
**Ice** Solid water
**Ice** takes the shape of the container.

❑

# F

1 **Faces** Accept/endure
*The robber **faces** many charges.*
**Fasces** Symbol of power
The king keeps a sceptre as **fasces**.

2 **Facet** Side
*We should look at all the **facets** of life.*
**Fact** Truth
He told me the **fact**.

3 **Facial** Of or for face
*This is a **facial** cream.*
**Facile** Easy
This sum seems very **facile**.

4 **Facilitate** Make easy
*Many machines **facilitate** our day-to-day work.*
**Felicitate** Congratulate
We have arranged a function to **felicitate** achievers.

5 **Facility** Ease
*What **facility** do you get from government for this project?*
**Felicity** Joy
It was great **felicity** for the old man to see the entire family.

6 **Factious** Inclined to groupism

*Your **factious** attitude is not good for our party.*

**Factitious** Artificial

Those flowers look real but they are **factitious**.

7 **Fad** Craze

*There is great **fad** for jeans all over the world.*

**Fade** Lose light

The lamp faded after some time.

**Fed** Give to eat

I **fed** the horse with gram.

8 **Fail** Don't succeed

*How did he **fail** in the final exam?*

**Fell** Knock down

The apple **fell** beside Newton.

9 **Faint** Unconscious

*The old lady **fainted** due to heat.*

**Feint** Attack

They will **feint** from behind.

10 **Fair** Lovely, just show

*It is a **fair** means.*

*Let us go to the **fair**.*

**Far** At a distance

Moon is very **far** from earth.

**Fare** Passage money, performance

What is the **fare** to Delhi?

How did you **fare** in exam?

11 **Fain** Gladly

*He would **fain** attend our function.*

**Feign** Pretend

Why did you **feign** sickness?

12 **Fairy** Lovely angel

*Grandma is telling a **fairy** tale.*

**Ferry** Boat

You can cross the river in a **ferry**.

13 **Fall** Come down freely

*How did the boy **fall**?*

**Foal** Young one of horse

The **foal** is running around its mother.

14 **Fallow** Uncultivated

*Scientists are trying the new fertilizer on **fallow** land.*

**Felloe** Outer circle

Draw a line touching the **felloe**.

**Fellow** Person

Why are you staring at that strange **fellow**?

15 **Falls** Water fall

*Have been to Niagara **falls**?*

**False** Untrue

What you say is **false**.

16 **Fan** An appliance

***Fan** is very useful during summer.*

**Fen** Wet place

You will spoil your shoes in that **fen**.

17 **Faster** Speedy
*Cheetah is **faster** than all other animals.*
**Foster** Bring up
The present system of education fails to **foster** the qualities of good citizen.

18 **Fat** Bulky
*Elephant is a **fat** animal.*
**Fate** Luck
Do you believe in **fate**?
**Fete** Celebration
There was a cultural **fete** in our college.

19 **Fatal** Which causes death
*Cancer is a **fatal** disease.*
**Fettle** Condition
We are passing through bad **fettle**.

20 **Favour** Approval
*Will the judge **favour** me?*
**Flavour** Taste
Have you tasted new **flavour** of ice-cream?

21 **Feast** Celebratory dinner
*There was a **feast** in our house on my birthday.*
**Fist** Fingers together
The officer hit the thief with his **fist**.

22 **Feat** An act of skill
*Jugglers perform great **feats**.*
**Feet** Part of body
His **feet** are wet.
**Fit** Proper
Have you found a **fit** person for this job?

23 **Feature** Characteristics

*He told me about the **features** of Europe.*

**Future** About to happen

He is investing for his son's **future**.

24 **Feel** Experience

*How do you **feel** now?*

**Fill** Block up

**Fill** this pot with water.

25 **Feral** Wild

*There are many **feral** plants beside the farm.*

**Ferial** Not festival

His experience was a matter of **ferial**.

**Ferrel** Part of stick

The **ferrel** of this stick is thin.

26 **Fern** Flowerless plant

*Why do you like to grow **ferns** in your garden?*

**Firm** Fixed, business concern

It is **firm** that he will meet us at the theatre.

He is the proprietor of an export **firm**.

27 **Feu** Strip of land

*We can cultivate crop in this **feu**.*

**Few** Not many

I have **few** rupees in bank.

**Phew** Expression of relief

**'Phew'** he said after reaching home safely.

28 **Fiction** Imaginative

*Do you like to read **fiction** novels?*

**Faction** Small group

A **faction** joined the opposition.

29 **Fiddle** Cheat
*That shopkeeper **fiddles** his customers.*
**Fuddle** Çonfuse
You should not **fuddle** children with difficult questions.

30 **Filch** Snatch
*The monkey may **filch** the loaf of bread from your hand.*
**Finch** A bird
Look at the flight of that **finch**.
**Flinch** Not sure
The new actor **flinched** before entering.

31 **Fir** A tree
*There are many **fir** trees in cold region.*
**Fur** Hair skin of animal
Animals are given **fur** for protection against cold.

32 **Fission** Divide into two
*The scientist can create **fission** of tissues.*
**Fusion** Mixture
We are trying to develop something new by **fusion** of two gases.

33 **Flagrant** Glaring
*You cannot escape punishment from this **flagrant** crime.*
**Fragrant** Sweet smelling
My new perfume is very **fragrant**.

34 **Flair** Ability
*He has a good **flair** of speech.*
**Flare** Burn
The silk **flared** up soon.

35 **Flak** Abuse

*How dare he **flak** us like that?*

**Flake** Piece of ice

Look at the **snowflakes** on the roof.

**Fleck** Dot on skin

There are many **flecks** on his face.

36 **Flatter** Compliment unduly

*He **flatters** his boss to get a raise.*

**Flutter** Flap wings

The kite does not **flutter** often.

37 **Flaunt** Display

*It is not good to **flaunt** money.*

**Flout** Mock

We should not **flout** that blind man.

38 **Flaw** Defect

*There is a **flaw** in this manufacturing process.*

**Flow** Move constantly

The Ganga **flows** all the year round.

39 **Flax** A plant

*What can you make from **flax**?*

**Flex** Bend

The gymnast can **flex** her body like rubber.

40 **Flea** An insect

*This crop should be protected from **flea**.*

**Flee** Run away

Deer will **flee** on seeing the tiger.

41 **Fleet** A group of ships

*The American **fleet** attacked Germany.*

**Flit** Come out

Guess, what will **flit** from this box.

42 **Flew** Fly away

*Birds **flew** on seeing men.*

**Flu** Illness

I had **flu** last week.

43 **Floor** Downside of house

*The **floor** is made of marble.*

**Flour** Churned grains

I prepared this food with wheat **flour**.

44 **Foam** Bubble

*This soap produces much **foam**.*

**Form** Shape, documents for information

The **form** of this article is beautiful.

You have to fill this **form** for admission.

45 **Font** Letter of computer

*What type of **font** do you want to use in your letter?*

**Fount** Spring of water

Mogul kings had many **founts** in their palace.

46 **Fool** Stupid

*Who is that **fool**?*

**Full** Complete

The hall is **full** of students.

47 **For** In interest of

*I work hard* ***for*** *earning.*

**Fore** Ahead

The donkey does not kick with its **fore** legs.

**Four** Digit

All animals have **four** legs.

48 **Foremast** Part of ship

*Sailors stand on* ***foremast*** *to find direction.*

**Foremost** Ahead

China is **foremost** in population.

49 **Formally** Ceremonious

*The minister* ***formally*** *greeted the visitors.*

**Formerly** Before

**Formerly,** I was an HR Manager in corporate.

50 **Fort** Protective wall

*Red* ***Fort*** *was protection for Delhi.*

**Forte** Quality

What do you say about **forte** of this medicine?

51 **Foul** Unfair

*Don't use* ***foul*** *means in the game.*

**Fowl** A bird

We saw a **fowl** in the zoo.

52 **Founded** Searched

*Ramkrishna mission was* ***founded*** *by Swami Vivekanand.*

**Foundered** Sink

All his efforts **foundered** on the rock of failure.

53 **Freeze** Experience extreme cold

*Our blood would **freeze** in Antarctica.*

**Fridge** An appliance

What is the price of your **fridge**?

**Frieze** Decoration on wall

They had called an expert of **frieze** in marriage function.

54 **Fuss** Commotion

*There was **fuss** in the Parliament on the new bill.*

**Fuzz** Fluff

Some dogs have thin **fuzz**.

❑

# G

1 **Gabble** — Talk fast

*Don't **gabble** like that, I can't understand.*

**Gable** — Triangular upper part of wall

The architect explained the plan of **gable** to the mason.

2 **Gaff** — Barbed fishing rod

*We are fishing with a **gaff**.*

**Gaffe** — Blunder

I made a **gaffe** in my business so bad to incur huge loss.

**Guff** — Empty talk

Don't **guff**; it is not a good habit.

3 **Gaily** — Happily

*They celebrated the function **gaily**.*

**Galley** — Vessel rowed by slaves

In ancient time, many slaves worked in **galley**.

4 **Gait** — Manner of walking

*Her **gait** is very graceful.*

**Gate** — Opening to enter

Where is the college **gate**?

**Get** — Achieve, receive

He must **get** the first prize.

5 **Gamble** Play for money

*Many persons **gamble** and ruin themselves.*

**Gambol** Dance or play

The young deer were **gambol** in the forest.

6 **Gaol** Prison

*The prisoner ran away from the **gaol**.*

**Goal** Aim

Is mere enjoyment the **goal** of life?

7 **Gap** Place

*There is some **gap** between two cars to park your scooter.*

**Gape** See with open mouth

The child **gaped** at the acrobats in circus.

8 **Garb** Clothing of special kind

*The **garb** of king is very costly.*

**Grab** Hold

We should **grab** this opportunity.

9 **Gargle** Wash throat

*Do you **gargle** with hot water?*

**Gurgle** Bubbling sound

Listen to the constant **gurgle** of river below.

10 **Garish** Gaudy

*I don't like such **garish** cloths.*

**Greyish** Colour

His pant is **greyish**.

11 **Garment** Ready-made cloths

*He wears fine **garments**.*

**Gourmet** Expert judge of food

The **gourmet's** decision was in favour of my dish.

| | | |
|---|---|---|
| 12 | **Gas** | Air-like substance |
| | *Hydrogen is a light **gas**.* | |
| | **Gaze** | See constantly |
| | Why are you **gazing** at stars? | |
| | **Guess** | Estimate |
| | **Guess** who is coming to meet us. | |
| 13 | **Gash** | Long deep cut or wound |
| | *He got a **gash** while reaping.* | |
| | **Gush** | Emit or flow in sudden stream |
| | Blood **gushed** from his wound. | |
| 14 | **Gauge** | Measurement of thickness of sheet |
| | *What is the **gauge** of this cupboard?* | |
| | **Gouge** | Chisel |
| | The artisan is carving with a **gouge**. | |
| 15 | **Gauss** | Unit of magnetic fluid density |
| | *The scientist is working about the **gauss**.* | |
| | **Gauze** | Thin fabric |
| | Can you make some garment from this **gauze**? | |
| 16 | **Gel** | Thin like water |
| | *The medicine is in* a ***gel** form.* | |
| | **Jail** | Prison |
| | There are many prisoners in this **jail**. | |
| | **Jell** | Take a definite form |
| | Water will **jell** in this vessel. | |
| 17 | **Gem** | Precious stone |
| | *His ring is studded with **gems**.* | |
| | **Germ** | Micro-organisms causing disease |
| | You can see **germs** under a microscope. | |

18 **Gene** Chromosome

*He has intellectual **genes** of his father.*

**Jeans** Denim

**Jeans** is the most popular garment in the world.

19 **Genteel** Well-bred

*He is the product of a **genteel** society.*

**Gentle** Polite

His behaviour towards us was **gentle**.

20 **Ghastly** Shocking

*It was a **ghastly** incident.*

**Ghostly** Like a ghost

The **ghostly** figure disappeared suddenly.

21 **Gilt** Cover thinly with gold

*She is wearing **gilt** bangles.*

**Guilt** Feeling of having done wrong

I feel **guilt** for insulting you.

22 **Gist** Essence of matter

*Tell me the **gist** of your discussion with your boss.*

**Jest** To joke

I like to **jest** with my friends.

23 **Glad** Happy

*I am **glad** you came.*

**Glade** Open space in forest

We will camp in this **glade**.

24 **Glair** White of egg

*Take out the **glair** and put it in this bowl.*

**Glare** Shine dazzlingly

I cannot endure the **glare** of sun.

25 **Gleam** Shine
*The moon **gleams** beautifully at night.*
**Glean** Acquire
He will **glean** much wealth with his product.

26 **Glebe** Land for clergyman
*The **glebe** was given to construct quarters.*
**Glib** Speak without sincerity
His **glib** communication is not good.

27 **Gnat** Two winged fly
*Close the windows or the **gnats** will enter.*
**Net** Open mesh fabric of rope
This **net** is made to protect us from mosquitoes.

28 **Goad** Irritate
*Don't **goad** me; I am not in good mood.*
**God** Almighty
**God** is everywhere.

29 **Goat** An animal
***Goat's** milk is good.*
**Got** Received
I **got** this medal in writing competition.
**Gout** A disease of joint
I must consult a good doctor for **gout**.

30 **Golf** A game
*I play **golf** every Sunday.*
**Gulf** Stretch of sea consisting of a deep inlet
The **gulf** of Cambay is in the west side of India.

31 **Golly** Expressing surprise

*"**Golly!**" he said on seeing me.*

**Gully** Water worn ravine

The boat has just turned into a **gully**.

32 **Grand** Big

*He lives in a **grand** house.*

**Grant** Allow

I will **grant** bonus to my servants.

33 **Grate** Fire place

*Fire is blazing in the **grate**.*

**Great** Big

Milton was a **great** poet.

34 **Greet** Welcome, meet

*I have come out to **greet** our guest.*

**Grit** Particles of stone or sand

**Grit** is often used in building.

35 **Grim** Harsh

*He is very **grim** with his enemies.*

**Grime** Dirt on surface

There is a project to clean the **grime** of this pond.

**Grin** Smile showing teeth

The child **grinned** at me on seeing a toy.

36 **Grip** Hold

***Grip** the racket tightly.*

**Gripe** Complain

Will you **gripe** my father about me?

37 **Grovel** Show extreme affection

*Why does he **grovel** his parents?*

**Growl** Animal's noise

The tiger **growled** at us from the cage.

38 **Guarantee** Formal promise of quality

*There is seven years **guarantee** on this T.V.*

**Guaranty** Thing serving as security

I gave my land as **guaranty** in bank.

❑

# H

1 **Hack** Cut roughly, common place

*Farmers **hack** grains from plant.*

**Hake** A fish

There is a **hake** in this pond.

**Heck** Mild exclamation of surprise

"**Heck**!" He said on seeing me.

2 **Hackle** Erected hair on animal's body

*Look at the **hackle** of this angry cat.*

**Heckle** Interrupt and harass

Why do you **heckle** in our programme?

3 **Had** Once owned

*I **had** many toys in childhood.*

**Head** Part of body

Helmet protects the **head**.

4 **Hail** Frozen raindrop

*Yesterday there was **hail-storm**.*

**Hale** Health

We are quite **hale** and hearty.

**Hell** Place of devils and sinners

I cursed him to go to **hell**.

5 **Hair** Part of head

*She has curly **hair**.*

**Hare** An animal

The **hare** lost race against turtle.

**Heir** Person receiving property

He is **heir** to his father's property.

6 **Hairy** Full of hair

*The bear is a **hairy** animal.*

**Harry** Harass

Don't **harry** that boy.

**Hurry** Haste

**Hurry** up, or we will be late.

7 **Hall** Big room

*The **hall** was full of people.*

**Haul** Pull or drag forcibly

He **hauled** the horse out of the stable.

**Hole** Empty space in solid body

Can you see anything from this **hole**?

**Whole** Entire

The child wants the **whole** pack of biscuit.

8 **Hallow** Make holy

*People have **hallowed** Gandhiji's image.*

**Halo** Circle of light surrounding the head of sacred person

There was a white **halo** behind the head of Lord Krishna.

9 **Ham** Upper part of pig's leg for food

***Ham** is eaten with bread in some countries.*

**Hem** Calling attention by cough

The child is **hemming** to call his father.

10 **Handmade** Made by hand
*These **handmade** articles are beautiful.*
**Handmaid** Female servant
Our **handmaid** is well trained and honest.

11 **Handsome** Good-looking
*Your son is very **handsome**.*
**Hansom** Two-wheeled cart
In village, many people travel by **hansom**.

12 **Harass** Trouble
*Please don't **harass** the dog.*
**Harness** Equipment to control fasten
A good jockey keeps his horse under **harness**.

13 **Hardly** Rarely
*I **hardly** work on weekends.*
**Hardy** Robust
This sportsman is very **hardy**.

14 **Hart** Male deer
*Two **harts** were fighting for food.*
**Heart** Part of body
**Heart** beats constantly.

15 **Has** Own
*Elephant **has** a short tail.*
**Haze** Thin atmosphere
Visibility is very low in **haze**.

16 **Hash** Mess
*He has made a **hash** in his room.*
**Hush** Become silent
The children were **hushed** when the guest arrived.

17 **Hat** Type of cap
*Variety of **hats** is worn all over the world.*
**Hate** Dislike
I **hate** religious fanaticism.

18 **Hatch** Incubate, device
*The hen will **hatch** some eggs soon.*
**Hutch** Cage for rabbits
Put some carrots in the **hutch**.

19 **Haunting** Linger in mind
*There are many **haunting** memories of my childhood.*
**Hunting** Kill or capture
**Hunting** was a favourite sport of kings.

20 **Haven** Refuge
*Pakistan has become a **haven** of terrorists and criminals.*
**Heaven** Paradise
Some places are like **heaven**.

21 **Hay** Dry grass
*The ox is eating **hay**.*
**Hey** Calling attention
'**Hey!**' said the child on seeing balloons.

22 **Heal** Cure
*How did your injury **heal** so fast?*
**Heel** Part of foot
This runner runs with support of **heels**.
**Hill** Small mountain
There is a temple on that **hill**.

23 **Heap** Pile
*There was a big **heap** of books in the library.*
**Hip** Part of body
The cyclist sits on the cycle on **hips**.

24 **Hear** Listen
*Did you **hear** the latest news?*
**Here** This place
He will come to meet us **here**.
**Hire** Rent
We will **hire** a taxi from here.

25 **Heard** Past tense of hear
*I **heard** a mysterious story.*
**Herd** Number of cattle
A **herd** of cows was grazing in the field.

26 **Hearsay** Rumour
*There was **hearsay** about the affair.*
**Heresy** Religious belief contrary to orthodox
Joan of Arc was burnt for **heresy**.

27 **Heat** High temperature
*There is much **heat** during summer.*
**Hit** Strike
The batsman **hits** the ball from ground.

28 **Heed** Attend
*He should **heed** your advice.*
**Hid** Keep away
The thief **hid** the money under a tree.

29 **Hemp** A plant
*Does **hemp** grow anywhere?*
**Hump** Round raised part on camel's back
We cannot sit on camel's **hump**.
**Humph** Sound of doubt
Why did you **humph** while I was talking?

30 **Hence** For this reason

*.....**Hence** we should be good citizens.*

**Hens** A bird

How many **hens** are in this poultry farm?

31 **Heroin** Narcotic drug

*He was caught with **heroin**.*

**Heroine** Main female character

Who is the **heroine** in this film?

32 **Hew** To cut down

*Do not **hew** the tree.*

**Hue** Noise, colour

He raised a **hue** and cry.

33 **Hi** Greet

*We say '**Hi**' to our friends.*

**High** Above the ground

Aeroplane can fly very **high**.

34 **His** Belonging to him

*That is **his** new bike.*

**Hiss** Voice of snake

This cobra is **hissing** angrily.

35 **Historical** Related to history

*The book is based on **historical** evidence.*

**Hysterical** Excitement

When I went to his house, I found him in **hysterical** state.

36 **Hoard** To store

*It is wicked to **hoard** grain, when the poor are starving.*

**Horde** Wandering tribe

The country was over-run by **hordes** of Turks.

37 **Hoarse** Rough voice
*I cannot take a lecture with this* ***hoarse*** *voice.*
**Horse** An animal
**Horse** is a very useful animal.

38 **Hoist** Hang
*The President of India will* ***hoist*** *the national flag.*
**Host** One who has guests
Mr. Anand will be our **host** in Mumbai.

39 **Hone** Shine and sharpen
*The warrior is* ***honing*** *his sword.*
**Horn** Noise of vehicle
Don't **horn** often.

40 **Honour** Respect
*We should* ***honour*** *our elders.*
**Owner** One to whom thing belongs
Who is the **owner** of this beautiful house?

41 **Hop** Small jump
*The monkey was* ***hopping*** *on the tree.*
**Hope** Expect
We **hope** to get better result.

42 **Hostel** Place for students to live
*This is the boys'* ***hostel*** *of our college.*
**Hostile** Opposed
How can we put up with his **hostile** nature?

43 **Hour** Time unit
*There are 24* ***hours*** *in a day.*
**Our** Belonging to us
This is **our** shop.

44 **Howl** Voice of fox, wolf

*Listen to the **howl** of jackal.*

**Owl** A bird

**Owl** is a nocturnal bird.

45 **Hull** Outer covering of ship

*The **hull** for the new ship is ready.*

**Hurl** Throw

Don't **hurl** stones at the dog.

46 **Human** Man

*We are **human** beings.*

**Humane** Kind

We must be **humane** in our manners.

47 **Humble** Modest

*I like his **humble** personality.*

**Umbel** Flower-cluster

Bees are flying around **umbel**.

48 **Humerus** Bone of upper arm

*There is a crack in his **humerus**.*

**Humorous** Jolly

Your friend is a **humorous** person.

❑

# I

1 **Ice** Frozen water
*There are many **ice** cubes in this thermos.*
**Icing** Coating of sugar
Put some **icing** on my cake.
**Icy** Very cold
There is **icy** water in Maan Sarovar.

2 **Ideal** Perfect
*Gandhiji was an **ideal** leader.*
**Idle** Lazy
You should leave your **idle** habits if you want to succeed.
**Idol** Image of God
It is a fine **idol** of Lord Krishna.
**Idyll** A poem
There are many lovely **idylls** written in English.

3 **Illegible** Unreadable handwriting
*If you write such **illegible** hand in the exam, you will get poor result.*
**Ineligible** Not qualified
He has been declared **ineligible** for promotion.

4 **Impatience** Haste
*Your **impatience** will not yield good results.*
**Impatiens** Plant
We have **impatiens** in our laboratory.

5 **Impeccable** Faultless
*He has an **impeccable** style of managing.*
**Implacable** Unable to calm
The wrath of nature is **implacable**.

6 **Imperial** Majestic
*Once upon a time this was an **imperial** court.*
**Imperil** Endanger
Many species of animals and birds are **imperiled**.

7 **Impetuous** Act rashly
*You should improve your **impetuous** nature.*
**Impetus** Impulse
On seeing him I had a sudden **impetus** of anger.

8 **Impossible** Not possible
*To control nature is **impossible** for human being.*
**Impassable** That cannot be passed
Why do you make such **impassable** suggestions?

9 **Imposter** Person who assumes false character
***Imposter** was arrested and put behind the bars.*
**Imposture** Deception
He will be punished for his **imposture**.

10 **In** A preposition
*Water is **in** the glass.*
**Inn** Place to live in
Travellers are resting in an **inn**.

11 **Incite** To arouse to action
*Netaji **incited** the masses to fight for freedom.*
**Insight** Capacity to understand
Sardar Patel was a man with a lot of **insight**.

12 **Indemnity** Compensation for damage
*I signed an **indemnity** before starting a project.*
**Identity** Condition or being specified person
Please reveal your **identity**.

13 **Indent** Make mark, impress
*I will **indent** in my school for my cleverness.*
**Intent** Have purpose
What do you **intent** to do after graduation?

14 **Indict** Accuse by legal process
*Why did you **indict** him for such a small matter?*
**Induct** Install
We have **inducted** more computers in our office.

15 **Indigent** Needy
*We should help the **indigent**.*
**Indignant** Angry
Don't show your **indignant** nature in office.

16 **Industrial** Related to industry
*India will soon become an **industrial** country.*
**Industrious** Hard working
Young man must be **industrious** to achieve success.

17 **In fact** Truly
***In fact**, I had called you to solve my problem.*
**Infect** Affect by germ
Dirty water will **infect** you with many diseases.

18 **Inflect** Change pitch of the voice
*We can **inflect** in the cassette by the help of this button.*
**Inflict** Impose
Hitler **inflicted** much harassment on Jews.

19 **Ingenuous** Noble

*He is admired for his **ingenuous** nature.*

**Ingenious** Clever

He invented a very **ingenious** plan for business promotion.

20 **Inhabit** Dwell

*Many wild animals **inhabit** in Africa.*

**Inhibit** Prevent

Government **inhibited** epidemic by much effort.

21 **Inherent** Existing as a permanent attribute

*"Mahatma" is an **inherent** title of Gandhiji.*

**Inherit** Receive by legal succession

He **inherited** much wealth.

22 **Insert** Put one thing into another

*Have you **inserted** CD in the player?*

**Inset** Extra section in a book

Look at the instructions in the **inset**.

23 **Instance** Example

*We can take many **instances** from the life of a good man.*

**Instant** Immediately

He replied in an **instant**.

24 **Intact** Undamaged

*We should keep old monuments **intact**.*

**Intake** To take in

Why did she **intake** a strong dose of medicine?

25 **Intensely** Very much

*Do you love her **intensely**?*

**Intentionally** Purposely

He had **intentionally** thrown the ball towards me.

26 **Interject** Interrupt
*Don't **interject** in my speech.*
**Intersect** Divide by crossing
**Intersect** this line from here.

27 **Intimation** Make known
*I have received **intimation** from government about my case.*
**Intimidation** Frighten, overawe
The officer will finish the matter by **intimidation**.

28 **Invert** Topple
*Why did you **invert** this chair?*
**Inward** Of inside
Do you enjoy **inward** peace?

29 **Irrelevant** Unnecessary
*Don't say **irrelevant** things.*
**Irreverent** Careless
His **irreverent** attitude is harmful.

30 **Irreplaceable** That cannot be replaced
*Loss of certain relations is **irreplaceable**.*
**Irrepressible** That cannot be repressed
Love is **irrepressible** feeling.

❑

# J

1 **Jab** Hit

*The boxer **jabbed** his rival.*

**Job** Work for money

He has a good **job**.

2 **Jalousie** Slatted blind to keep out light, rain

*Put the **jalousie** at noon to keep away the sunlight.*

**Jealousy** Envy

He bears **jealousy** against me.

3 **Jangle** Make a metallic sound

*Don't **jangle** with spoon and dish.*

**Jungle** Forest

**Jungles** should be preserved and protected.

4 **Jealous** Envious

*Beware of **jealous** people.*

**Zealous** Enthusiastic

His **zealous** nature got him a good name.

5 **Jest** To joke

*I like to **jest** with friends.*

**Zest** Relish, enthusiasm

His **zest** for life is great.

6 **Jiggle** Shake or jerk light
*Please don't **jiggle** the table while I am writing.*
**Jingle** Sound of bell
I like the **jingle** during Christmas.

7 **Join** Unite
*Would you like to **join** us for dinner?*
**Joint** Point at which two things fit together
There are many **joints** in a human body.

8 **Judicial** Related to justice
*The **judicial** court will decide this case.*
**Judicious** Wise
His style of talking is very **judicious**.

9 **Junction** Joining point
My town is a railway **junction**.
**Juncture** Critical point of time
We will have to think twice before taking decision at this **juncture**.

**Jut** Protrude
A rod is **jutting** out of this carriage.
**Jute** A plant
There is good cultivation of **jute** in Bengal.

# K

1 **Keel** Place for launching boat
*Today there were many workers at the* ***keel****.*
**Kill** Create death forcefully
Hitler **killed** many innocent people.

2 **Keen** Enthusiastic
*The child is very* ***keen*** *to learn new games.*
**Kin** Young ones
Everyone cares for **kin**.

3 **Keep** Preserve
*I* ***keep*** *money in my wallet.*
**Kip** Sleep
I will take a short **kip**.

4 **Kinetic** Of or due to motion
*We feel breeze on vehicle due to* ***kinetic*** *energy.*
**Kinetics** Branch of physical chemistry
We have a paper of **kinetics** in our syllabus.

5 **Knack** Skill
*He has a good* ***knack*** *of teaching.*
**Neck** Part of body
We tie a strap around the **neck** of our dog.

6 **Knave** Fool
*He is **knave** to do such a thing.*
**Naïve** Innocent
I like his **naïve** nature.
**Nave** Central part of a church
Many devotees were worshipping, standing at the **nave**.

7 **Knead** Mix flour
*Our cook can **knead** in no time.*
**Need** Necessity of thing
I **need** your help.

8 **Knee** Part of body
*My stocking are till **knees**.*
**Neigh** Voice of horse
My pet horse will **neigh** on seeing me.

9 **Kneel** Fall on knees
*The disciple **kneels** on seeing the master.*
**Nil** Zero
His score was **nil** in last match.

10 **Knew** Had information
*I **knew** the result.*
**New** Fresh
Your **new** shirt is very good.

11 **Knight** High ranking soldier
*The **knight** fought bravely in battle.*
**Night** Time unit
We sleep at **night**.

12 **Knit** Make a garment
*She **knits** sweater every year.*
**Neat** Clean
I keep my room **neat**.

13 **Knob** Rounded piece to hold

*There are many designs for **knob**.*

**Nob** Person of wealth or high social position

Your friend is a **nob**.

14 **Knot** Intertwining of ropes

*Tie a **knot** here.*

**Not** Nothing

She didn't speak to me—**not** one word.

**Note** To record

We **note** down points from the lecture.

15 **Knotty** Difficult

*I can solve this **knotty** problem.*

**Naughty** Mischievous

That child is very **naughty**.

16 **Know** Have information

*I **know** the answer of this question.*

**No** Refuse

My answer is '**no**' to your proposal.

❑

# L

1 **Label** Piece of paper, etc.
*What is written on the **label**?*
**Labial** Of the lips
His pronunciations are mostly **labial**.

2 **Lac** Resinous substance
*This bangle is made of **lac**.*
**Lace** Shoe string
Tie the **lace** properly or you will fall.
**Lass** Girl
Who was that **lass** with you?

3 **Lack** Something less
***Lack** of manners and politeness is not good.*
**Lake** Pond
There are many fishes in this **lake**.

4 **Lad** Boy
*That **lad** is hard working.*
**Lade** Ship
Let us **lade** it with cotton.
**Laid** Past participle of lay
He has **laid** a mat there.
**Led** Make others follow
Napolean **led** the French army to many victories.
**Lead** A mineral
**Lead** is a useful mineral.

5 **Laden** Loaded

*The cart is **laden** with vegetables.*

**Leaden** Heavy or slow

This cart is very **leaden**.

6 **Lag** Fall behind

*Why did he **lag** in studies?*

**Leg** Part of body

Deer has thin long **legs**.

7 **Lam** Thrash

*He **lamed** the ball strongly.*

**Lame** Disabled in the leg

He cannot walk fast because he is **lame**.

8 **Lamp** Appliance giving light

*It is getting dark, please light the **lamp**.*

**Lump** Quantity of

Put a **lump** of salt in this dish.

9 **Land** Stretch of earth

*This **land** is reserved for farming.*

**Lend** Give for use

Bank can **lend** you money to buy a new house.

10 **Lane** Street

*In which **lane** is your house?*

**Line** Continuous mark made on surface

Draw a vertical **line** from this point.

11 **Late** After time

*Why are you **late** for the meeting?*

**Let** Allow

I will **let** him in if he shows the ticket.

12 **Later** — More late in time

*He came **later** than I did.*

**Latter** — Second of two things

Of gold and iron, the **latter** is more useful.

**Letter** — Written message

I shall write **letters** to you regularly.

13 **Lath** — Thin strip of wood

*This **lath** is useless, throw it.*

**Lathe** — Machine for shaping

I am working on a **lathe**.

14 **Lather** — Froth

*Wash the **lather** from your face.*

**Leather** — Material made from the skin of an animal

They are **leather** shoes.

15 **Law** — Rules of government

*All citizens should obey the **law**.*

**Low** — Downward

Share prices have gone **low** because of recession.

16 **Lay** — Place on a surface

*How many eggs did the hen **lay**?*

**Lie** — Speak untruth

I cannot believe that he would **lie** to me.

**Lye** — Water made alkaline by wood ashes

Can we use this **lye** for our research work?

17 **Leak** — Passing through

*How did the pipe **leak**?*

**Lick** — Pass the tongue over

I like to **lick** the candy.

18 **Leap** Jump
*The kangaroos took a big **leap**.*
**Lip** Part of face
His face bears high chick bones with pooped **lips**.

19 **Least** Too less
*Who has got the **least** marks?*
**List** Number of items
I have prepared a **list** of guests to be invited.

20 **Leave** Ask permission
*They will **leave** our house tomorrow.*
**Leaves** Part of tree
**Leaves** of different trees have different shapes.
**Live** To be alive
May you **live** happily!

21 **Lessen** To decrease
***Lessen** your worries and enjoy.*
**Lesson** Home work
Come with your **lesson** tomorrow.

22 **Levee** Landing place
*We will get down from the boat on **levee**.*
**Levy** Impose
Government will **levy** heavy tax after the war.

23 **Lever** Projecting handle
*Pull this **lever** to open.*
**Liver** Part of body
**Liver** should be protected from infection.

24 **Liable** Responsible
*Who is **liable** for this damage?*
**Libel** Publish false statement
This **libel** is not good for our reputation.

25 **Lid** Thing for covering mouth of vessel

*Remove the **lid** and see what is in.*

**Lead** Initiate

Who will **lead** our team to victory this time.

26 **Lightening** Making light

*Your support will help me in **lightening** my burden.*

**Lightning** Electric discharge

A flash of **lightning** appeared in the sky.

27 **Lion** An animal

***Lion** is the king of jungle.*

**Loin** Part of leg

Gandhiji used to wear **loin** cloth.

28 **Lips** Part of face

*Apply this cream on your dry **lips**.*

**Lisp** Speech defect

He **lisps** much.

29 **Litre** Unit of measurement

*Camel can drink many **litres** of water at a stretch.*

**Litter** Rubbish

Don't throw the **litter** here.

30 **Loath** Unwilling

*She is **loath** to join us.*

**Loathe** Hate

I **loathe** traitors of India.

31 **Loess** Deposit of fine windblown soil

*We can grow good crop in this **loess**.*

**Loss** No profit

He had to suffer a heavy **loss** due to fire in the factory.

32 **Look out** Keep watch

***Look out*** *for a taxi.*

**Outlook** Point of view

It is not my **outlook** how you should behave.

33 **Loose** Not right

*My shirt is **loose** at the shoulders.*

**Lose** Have no more

How did you **lose** your ring?

34 **Lore** Story

*There are many love **lores** famous in our region.*

**Lorn** Desolate

His **lorn** condition worries me.

35 **Lost** Cease to have

*He **lost** his watch.*

**Lots** Much

Our company bought this item in **lots**.

36 **Luxuriant** Strong in growth

*You have **luxuriant** hair.*

**Luxurious** Much comfort

Akbar led a **luxurious** life.

❑

# M

1 **Mace** Staff of authority

*Kings used to sit on throne holding a **mace**.*

**Mess** Place to dine

There was a **mess** in the kitchen.

2 **Mach** Unit of speed

*Fighter pilots can fly at 2-3 **mach**.*

**Make** Prepare

I shall **make** arrangements for your tour.

3 **Macron** Mark over a vowel

*You should look out for **macrons** in a dictionary to find out the exact pronunciation.*

**Micron** Unit of measurement

It is difficult to measure in small unit like **micron**.

4 **Mad** Insane

*The **mad** man was admitted to the mental hospital.*

**Made** Prepared

Who **made** this plan of my new bungalow?

**Maid** Young lady

He married a **maid** from the royal family.

5 **Mail** Letter
*I received his **mail** yesterday.*
**Male** Man
He has two **male** children.

6 **Maim** Disable
*Loss of this order can **maim** our business.*
**Main** Chief
Who has played the **main** role in this film?
**Man** Male human
Who is that **man**?
**Mane** Long hair of animal
The lioness has no **mane**.

7 **Mainly** Chiefly
*Who was **mainly** responsible for this damage?*
**Manly** Befitting a man
He showed his **manly** courage during the crisis.

8 **Maize** Corn
*I like the taste of baked **maize**.*
**Maze** Network
Don't get lost in this **maze** of words.

9 **Malady** Sickness
*There is no medicine for this **malady**.*
**Melody** Sweet music
Who could have composed such a fine **melody**?

10 **Malaise** Discomfort
*Let not such a simple thing **malaise** you.*
**Malice** Jealousy
He spoke about me out of **malice**.

11 **Mall** Cluster of shops
*I went to the **mall** for shopping.*
**Maul** Damage by criticism
*Why do you like to **maul** my name?*
**Mole** Birth mark on body
A **mole** under your lips gives you a good look.
**Moll** Prostitute
Police should curb the **moll** business.

12 **Mallow** A plant
*Have you seen the **mallow** in our garden?*
**Mellow** Soft
I like this **mellow** chewing-gum.

13 **Malt** Barley
*He has a farm of **malt**.*
**Melt** Make liquid
Ice **melts** easily.

14 **Manage** Organize
*I can **manage** my company without your help.*
**Manege** Area where horses are trained
There are some foals in the **manege** with their trainers.

15 **Manner** Style
*I like his **manner** of dealing with problems.*
**Manor** Large house
The estate owner lives in a **manor**.

16 **Mansion** Big house
*Our ancestral **mansion** was on a hill.*
**Mention** Refer
Please, do not **mention** his name.

17 **Mantel** Shelf over fine-place
*Place this clock on the **mantel**.*
**Mantle** Loose sleeveless cloak
He puts on a silk **mantle** at night.
**Mental** Related to mind
If you drink much, you will lose your **mental** balance.

18 **Mar** Spoil
*Anger **mars** his character.*
**Mare** She-horse
It is easy to ride a **mare**.
**Mere** Only
He lost the game by **mere** two points.

19 **Mare** She-horse
*The bridegroom is riding a **mare**.*
**Mayor** Head of corporation
Who is the **Mayor** of Bombay?

20 **Marital** Related to marriage
*His **marital** view is very orthodox.*
**Martial** Warlike
Rajput was a **martial** race.

21 **Marrow** Substance in bone
*This injection should reach his **marrow**.*
**Narrow** Not broad
His ideas about relations are very **narrow**.

22 **Marry** To wed
*She will not **marry** before completing her education.*
**Merry** Be happy
Eat, drink and be **merry**.

23 **Mash** Crushed mixture
*Bake this potato **mash** in oven.*
**Mass** Large number
A **mass** movement is necessary to stop corruption.

24 **Mast** Pole of ship
*A sailor has climbed on the **mast** to keep a watch.*
**Must** Necessity
We **must** obey the traffic rules.

25 **Masterful** Boasting
*He lost many friends due to his **masterful** nature.*
**Masterly** Skilful
Bruce Lee was **masterly** in martial arts.
**Mastery** Dominance
**Mastery** in any art requires too much practice.

26 **Mat** Cloth to sit on floor
*You can lie down on this **mat**.*
**Mate** Friend
I have helpful **mates** in office.
**Met** Saw
Who **met** you in the market?

27 **Matter** Thing
*They used soft **matter** to prepare this item.*
**Mutter** Speak slowly, not clearly
Don't **mutter** in the classroom.

28 **Meal** Lunch/dinner
*I will reset after **meal**.*
**Mill** A factory
Many workers are working in this **mill**.

39 **Mean** Small-minded
*I know that he is a very **mean** person.*
**Means** Device
You should not use wrong **means** to earn.

30 **Meant** Have meaning
*He **meant** to help us.*
**Mint** A plant, prepare coins
This is **mint** flavoured chewing-gum.
Do you know where they **mint** coins?

31 **Meat** Flesh
*Does she take **meat**?*
**Meet** To see
I shall **meet** you on Saturday.
**Mete** To allot
Roll numbers were **meted** to the students.
**Mitt** A glove
Put on this **mitt** before holding that hot bowl.

32 **Medal** Token of reward
*Ruby won a gold **medal** in swimming competition.*
**Meddle** To interfere
Do not **meddle** in my affairs.

33 **Median** In middle
*They should take a **median** view to solve this problem.*
**Medium** Thing for communication
Phone is the best **medium**.

34 **Meter** Instrument of measuring
*We have installed two **meters** in our house.*
**Metre** Unit of measurement
Give me three **metres** of cloth.

35 **Metal** Hard substance
*Iron is the most useful **metal**.*
**Mettle** Power, spirit
Every problem tests our **mettle**.

36 **Mewl** Sound of cat
*Why is your cat **mewling**?*
**Mule** An animal like horse
**Mule** is used in hilly regions.

37 **Midst** In middle
*We were trapped in the **midst** of storm.*
**Mist** Fog
I like to see the **mist** at hill stations.

38 **Might** Strength
*We can test our **might** in this race.*
**Mite** Small unit of money
I have a collection of **mite** coins.

39 **Milestone** Stone showing distance
*Please read the next **milestone**.*
**Millstone** Stone of mill
The miller is changing the **millstone**.

40 **Milliner** Who sells lady's hats
*The **milliner** at the corner has some good varieties.*
**Millionaire** Very rich
Who doesn't like to be a **millionaire**?

41 **Million** Unit of money/measurement
*There are **millions** of educated people in India.*
**Mullion** Vertical bar
Remove this **mullion** from here.

42 **Miner** One who works in mine
***Miners** have a miserable life.*
**Minor** Small, under age
He is **minor,** so he cannot vote.
It is a **minor** thing to worry about.

43 **Minuet** Song for dance
*Put on a **minuet** for the dance.*
**Minute** Unit of time, very small
I will return within twenty **minutes**.
In few hours, the **minute** army would be over thrown.

44 **Miscellaneous** Unimportant things
*I proved that I am not **miscellaneous** in the office.*
**Miscellany** Book of articles
Have you read this **miscellany**?

45 **Missal** Book of prayer
*I forgot my **missal** in the temple.*
**Missile** Weapon
This aircraft can carry many **missiles**.

46 **Mistral** Wind
*Small boats should beware of **mistral**.*
**Mistrial** Invalid trial
The judge warned the lawyer for **mistrial**.

47 **Moan** Show pain
*I could not see the **moan** of that helpless child.*
**Mourn** Regret for dead
Let us **mourn** together for our brave soldiers.

48 **Modal** Mood of verb
*Use the **modals** properly in your sentence.*
**Model** Representation
I saw the new **model** of Audi.

49 **Moment** Brief portion of time
*On hearing the news, I was shocked for a **moment**.*
**Movement** To move
Our spies will inform about enemy's **movement**.

50 **Momentary** Short-lived
*We experienced a **momentary** earthquake.*
**Momentous** Important
The board of directors took a **momentous** decision.

51 **Mop** Cloth to clean
*You must change the **mop**, this one has become dirty.*
**Mope** Depressed
Loss in business has left my father in **mope** condition.

52 **Moral** Lesson to learn
*What is the **moral** of this story?*
**Morale** Spirit
I shall never let my **morale** down.

53 **Morass** Confusion
*Tell me, how to get out of this **morass**.*
**Morose** Gloomy
Why are you in **morose** condition?

54 **More** Greater in quantity
*She scored **more** marks than her brother.*
**Mores** Customs
We have to change many social **mores** in our world.

55 **Morning** Early part of day
*We go for walk in the **morning**.*
**Mourning** Regret on death
The nation observed a day of **mourning** on the death of the leader.

56 **Morse** Code of letters
*Can you read this **Morse** code?*
**Moss** Flowerless plant
**Moss** has to be cleared from this pond.

57 **Mortar** Instrument for crushing food
*Please crush these nuts in **mortar**.*
**Motor** A machine
We lift water from the well with the help of **motor**.

58 **Motif** Theme in art
*What was the **motif** of that painting?*
**Motive** Tending to act
Money **motive** makes all work.

59 **Motel** Road side hotel
*It is a long drive; we shall have to pass one night in a **motel**.*
**Mottle** Marked with spots
Write a word in this **mottled** paper.

60 **Muck** Dirt
*There is so much **muck** around.*
**Murk** Darkness
Cats can see very well in **murk**.

61 **Muscat** Sweet wine
*This **muscat** tastes well.*
**Mascot** Animal bringing luck
What was the **mascot** of last Olympic?

❑

# N

1 **Nap** Short sleep
*Take a **nap**, it will refresh you.*
**Nape** Back of neck
Don't hit on the **nape**, it is dangerous.

2 **Naval** Related to navy
*My brother is a **naval** officer.*
**Navel** Part of body
The doctor gave injections around the **navel**.

3 **Navvy** Labourer involved in digging
*This well was dug by an expert **navvy**.*
**Navy** Body of ships for war
Uniform of the **navy** is white.

4 **Neap** Least tide
*Fishermen sailed as there is **neap** tide today.*
**Nip** Pinch
If you **nip** the baby, he will cry.

5 **Neat** Clean
*We must keep our surroundings **neat**.*
**Nit** Egg of louse
You can see this **nit** under a microscope.

6 **Negligent** Careless
*We must not be* ***negligent*** *citizens.*
**Negligible** Very little
There is a **negligible** difference between the twins.

7 **Need** Requirement
*I* ***need*** *some money to buy a new house.*
**Needs** Required things
Food, cloth and shelter are the basic **needs** of a human being.

8 **Neigh** Voice of horse
*Horse will* ***neigh*** *if you go near it.*
**Nigh** Near
The end of his dictatorship is **nigh**.

9 **Nib** Pen-point
*This pen has a sharp* ***nib****.*
**Nibs** Mocking title
Ravi got many **nibs** in the class because of his behaviour.

10 **Nice** Beautiful
*She lives in a* ***nice*** *house.*
**Niece** Relative
How old is your **niece**?

11 **Nobble** Try to win unfairly
*The team was disqualified on the charge of* ***nobbling****.*
**Noble** Good, kind
Our teacher is a **noble** person.

12 **Nod** Move head
*Why did he* ***nod*** *at us?*
**Node** Part of plant
There is an insect sitting on the **node**.

13 **Noisy** Which creates sound
*Your old car is very **noisy**.*
**Nosy** Inquisitive
His **nosy** nature irritates me.

14 **None** Nothing
***None** of us have any car.*
**Nun** Woman who has renounced the world
I got this religious sermon from a **nun**.

15 **Noose** Loop
*The running deer was trapped in a **noose**.*
**Nose** Part of body
Indian women wear a ring on **nose**.

16 **Nozzle** Mouth of a tube
*Put your thumb on the **nozzle** to spray water.*
**Nuzzle** Rub gently with nose
The child likes to **nuzzle** the puppy.

❑

# O

1 **Oaf** Stupid

*He proved himself an **oaf** by his acts.*

**Of** Belonging to

The role **of** teacher is very important.

**Off** Away

She can take a day **off** from her busy schedule.

2 **Oar** Used for rowing boat

*Use your **oars** fast.*

**Ore** A mineral

Karnataka has rich **ores** of gold.

**Or** Option

He will settle in Bombay **or** Delhi.

3 **Oat** A cereal

*This cake is made of **oat**.*

**Oath** Swearing

I took the **oath** in the court.

4 **Observe** Look attentively

*The coach is **observing** the movement of players.*

**Obverse** Opposite side

Who is sitting **obverse** to you?

5 **Occur** Happen
*The solar eclipse will **occur** at mid-day tomorrow.*
**Ochre** Earth of red colour
Paint this pot with **ochre**.

6 **Odd** Strange
*It was an **odd** act.*
**Odds** Variance
We will fight against all **odds** to achieve our goal.
**Ode** Lyric poem
Keats wrote beautiful **odes**.

7 **Official** Related to office
*I am on **official** duty.*
**Officious** To forward in offering services
His **officious** manner has made him unpopular.

8 **On** Above
*Sit **on** this sofa.*
**Own** To have ownership
I **own** a big house in village.

9 **Once** One time
*I have met him only **once**.*
**One** First digit
I have **one** brother.

10 **Ordinance** Law made by government
*The president has issued a new **ordinance**.*
**Ordnance** Cannon
**Ordnance** was fired on the enemy during war.

11 **Origan** Wild flower
*These **origan** plants are growing fast.*
**Origin** Starting point
Do you know the **origin** of Ganga.

12 **Ought** Expressing duty

*You **ought** to work hard.*

**Oust** Drive out

We shall **oust** him if he doesn't work.

**Out** Away from place

I was **out** of my office for the whole day.

❑

# P

1 **Pack** Tie collection of things
*They will deliver this **pack** by speed post.*
**Peck** Strike with beak
The sparrow is **pecking** on the mirror.

2 **Paddle** Row
***Paddle** your boat fast.*
**Peddle** Sell goods
He **peddles** new products from village to village.
**Puddle** Small pool
Walk away from the **puddle**.

3 **Pail** Vessel
*We collect milk into a **pail**.*
**Pale** Without colour
Why do you look **pale** today?

4 **Pain** Suffering
*I have a severe **pain** in my shoulder.*
**Pane** Sheet of glass in window
The ball broke the window **pane**.
**Pen** Instrument for writing
Do not use red **pen** in exam.

5 **Paint** To colour

*What colour will you* ***paint*** *your house?*

**Pant** Breath short and quick

He is **panting** because he had a brisk run.

**Pent** Shut in

On seeing me his **pent-up** feelings will rise.

6 **Pair** Set of two

*I bought a* ***pair*** *of new sports shoes.*

**Par** Degree

His performance was **par** excellence.

**Pare** To cut

Why don't you **pare** your hair?

7 **Palace** Big house of king

*There are many* ***palaces*** *in Rajasthan.*

**Palais** Public dance hall

She is going to perform at the **palais**.

8 **Palate** Inside of mouth

*This food itches in my* ***palate****.*

**Palette** Board for mixing colour

The artist has dropped the **palette**.

**Pallet** Grass bed

If you sleep on the **pallet** you won't feel cold.

**Pellet** Ball of bread

Prepare a few **pellets** with clean hands.

9 **Pall** Bored

*His talk* ***palls*** *me.*

**Pole** Long stick

He jumped over the wall with the help of a **pole**.

**Poll** Voting

Who will win the assembly **poll**?

10 **Paltry** Worthless

*I am not interested in your **paltry** matters.*

**Poultry** Domestic fowls

They have a good business of **poultry**.

11 **Paper** Material to write on

*I am writing on **paper**.*

**Pepper** Eatable spice

Sprinkle some **pepper** on the bread.

12 **Parch** Hot and dry

*I don't like to eat **parched** biscuit.*

**Perch** Bar for bird to rest

We have got a golden **perch** for our parrot.

13 **Parish** Local area

*There is a meeting of the **parish** committee today.*

**Perish** Ruin

Many species of animals have **perished** from our planet.

14 **Parry** Deal skilfully

*He **parried** with his competitors.*

**Perry** A drink

Have you anytime tasted **Perry**?

15 **Parson** Clergyman

*I met the **parson** for some advice.*

**Person** Individual human

Who is that **person**?

16 **Paste** Moist fairly stiff mixture

*I clean my teeth with a **paste**.*

**Pest** Troublesome thing

Some insects are **pest** to the crops.

17 **Pastor** Minister of Church
*He retired as a **pastor**.*
**Pester** Trouble
Do not **pester** the sleeping dog.

18 **Pat** Hit slightly for affection
*My dog likes to be **patted**.*
**Pet** Tamed animal/bird
We have a **pet**.

19 **Patrol** Guard
*Soldiers **patrol** the border even in night.*
**Petrol** Oil, fuel
The **petrol** price increases often.

20 **Paten** Shallow dish
*I cannot eat comfortably from this **paten**.*
**Patten** Shoe with raised sole
In America, cowboys wear **patten**.
**Pattern** Model
Did you like this **pattern** of embroidery?

21 **Paunch** Belly
*You should reduce your **paunch**.*
**Pouch** Small bag
Keep the money in the **pouch**.

22 **Peace** Quiet
*I like the **peace** of this place.*
**Piece** Part
Take a **piece** of chalk to write.
**Piss** Go away
**Piss** off from here.
**Peas** A food
She will cook **peas** for dinner.

23 **Peak** Highest point

*Everest is the highest mountain **peak**.*

**Peek** Sly look

Beware of his habit of **peeking**.

**Pick** Choose carefully

Commander will **pick** the best men for the mission.

24 **Peal** Loud sound

*There was a **peal** of laughter after the joke.*

**Peel** Take off the skin

**Peel** the potatoes and bake them.

**Pill** Medicine

I took a **pill** as I had fever.

25 **Pear** A fruit

*I have some **pears** for you.*

**Peer** Look closely

**Peer** in it and you will find what you want.

26 **Pearl** Costly things from oyster

*Necklace of **pearls** is very costly.*

**Purl** Flow with babbling sound

I like to listen the **purling** of river.

27 **Pedal** Part of cycle

*I have **pedal** brake in my cycle.*

**Peddle** Sell goods

He **peddles** from town to town.

28 **Peep** Look through narrow opening

*It is not good habit to **peep** inside someone's private room.*

**Pip** Seed of fruit

Take out the **pip** before eating.

29 **Pendant** Hanging jewel

*This **pendant** is studded with diamond.*

**Pendent** Undecided

I want to know about the **pendent** matters.

30 **Perfect** Complete

*This suit looks **perfect** on you.*

**Prefect** Captain in school

Our **prefect** believes in imposing discipline.

31 **Permeate** Pass through pour

*In the earthen vessel, the water **permeates** and evaporates.*

**Permit** Allow

I got the **permit** for game from principal.

**Permute** Interchange

The programme was **permuted** due to time factor.

32 **Perpetrate** Commit

*He should not **perpetrate** such a mistake.*

**Perpetuate** To continue

Let us donate a yearly prize to **perpetuate** the memory of our grandfather.

33 **Persecute** To trouble

*Why did you want to **persecute** your poor debtor?*

**Prosecute** To pursue

I shall **prosecute** my studies after my illness.

34 **Personal** One's own

*What is your **personal** opinion?*

**Personnel** Persons employed

This compartment is reserved for army **personnel**.

35 **Perquisite** Privilege
*In a democratic state, there should not be* ***perquisite*** *for any class or caste.*
**Prerequisite** Essential
Do you possess all the **prerequisite** knowledge and experience for this job?

36 **Peruse** Examine, read carefully
*I was* ***perusing*** *my office accounts.*
**Pursue** Run after
The policemen **pursued** the gangster to his den.

37 **Petty** Small matter
*We should not argue over* ***petty*** *things.*
**Piety** Being pious
He is respected because of his **piety**.
**Pity** Kindness
I took **pity** on the injured animal and helped it.

38 **Physic** Medicine
*What* ***physic*** *do you take to cure fever?*
**Physics** Branch of science
Newton is regarded as father of **physics**.
**Physique** Bodily health
He has a sturdy **physique**.

39 **Pile** Heap
*You can search your notebook in that* ***pile****.*
**Piles** Sickness
He has consulted an expert doctor for his problem of **piles**.

40 **Pin** Small and thin pointed rod
*Pass a* ***pin*** *through these papers.*
**Pine** A tree, long for
There are many **pines** on hill station.
The old lady **pines** to see her daughter.

41 **Plain** Simple

*I believe in **plain** living and high thinking.*

**Plane** Flying vehicle

You can reach any part of the world in short time in a **plane**.

42 **Plan** Design

*The **plan** of your factory is very good.*

**Plant** Shrub

Which is that **plant** with orange flowers?

43 **Plausible** Probable

*It is **plausible** that India will become superpower.*

**Possible** Capable of being done

It is not **possible** for us to fly like birds.

44 **Plum** A fruit

*This **plum** is not ripe yet.*

**Plume** Large feather

Which bird's **plume** is this?

45 **Plus** Sign of addition

*Read carefully the points with **plus** marks.*

**Plush** Cloth material

From where did you get this **plush**?

46 **Poach** Hunt illegally

***Poaching** should be stopped.*

**Porch** Entrance of a house

This furniture is for **porch**.

47 **Pool** Small body of water

*Let's fish in this **pool**.*

**Pull** Exert force

**Pull** to open the door.

48 **Poppet** Dainty person
*My younger sister is the **poppet** of our family.*
**Puppet** Small figure moved by strings
There was a **puppet** show in our village.

49 **Popular** Liked by all
*Amitabh Bachchan is a very **popular** actor.*
**Populous** Thickly populated
India is a **populous** country.

50 **Pore** Small hole
*A bath helps to keep the **pores** open.*
**Pour** Cause flow
**Pour** out some coffee in my cup, please.

51 **Porter** Coolie
*The **porter** will carry your luggage downstairs.*
**Potter** One who makes pots
The **potter** has given good shape to this pot.

52 **Portion** Part
*This **portion** of the hall is used to keep things.*
**Potion** Dose of medicine
You will have to take bigger **potion** for speedy recovery.

53 **Poster** Printed picture
*Where shall we hang this **poster**?*
**Posture** Stance
His sitting **posture** is uncomfortable.

54 **Practical** Of use in practice
***Practical** knowledge is more important.*
**Practicable** Which can be used
A trip to the outer space has become **practicable**.

55 **Praise** Give compliments
*Beware of persons who **praise** much.*
**Press** Exert force on
**Press** the lid to close the jar.

56 **Pray** Offer words to God
*I **pray** to God everyday.*
**Prey** Hunt and kill
Tiger is a beast of **prey**.

57 **Precede** To go before
*My name **precedes** yours in the list.*
**Proceed** To go on
You can **proceed** in your research.

58 **Précis** Summary
*Tell me the **précis** of your essay.*
**Precise** Exact
You should be very **precise** in your decision.

59 **Premier** First in position
*Mr. Nehru was the first **premier** of India.*
**Premiere** First performance
The Season premiere of my favourite show is coming soon.

60 **Premise** House, property
*We have built a wall around our **premise**.*
**Premiss** Previous statement
I am talking about your **premiss**.

61 **Prescribe** Recommend
*My teacher has **prescribed** a book of grammar for practice.*
**Proscribe** To ban
The government has **proscribed** many anti-social activities.

62 **Presentiment** Previous apprehension
*The mother's actions were due to **presentiment**.*
**Presentment** Accusation
Serious allegations against the accused called for **presentment** by the Supreme Court.

63 **Price** Value
*What is the **price** of this car?*
**Prize** Reward
He has won a **prize** in school function.

64 **Principal** Head of school or college
*Our **principal** is a popular figure in the town.*
**Principle** Doctrine
I prefer to sacrifice money rather than **principle**.

65 **Pure** Unmixed
*It is difficult to get **pure** food nowadays.*
**Puree** Pulp of fruit of vegetable
You can add tomato **puree** for taste.

66 **Pulse** Throbbing of artery
*His **pulse** rate has become stable now.*
**Pulses** Eatable
We cook **pulses** regularly.

❑

# Q

1 **Quack** Unqualified doctor

*The system of **quacks** was harmful in olden times.*

**Quake** Tremble

There are many reasons which cause **earthquake**.

2 **Quarry** Mine of stones

*Many workers work in that **quarry** from morning to night.*

**Query** Question

If you have any **query**, you can ask.

3 **Quiet** Silent

*All is **quiet** at night.*

**Quite** Altogether

His performance is **quite** good.

4 **Quill** Feather

*Peacock has colourful **quills**.*

**Quilt** Sheet for covering body

We use **quilt** during winter.

❑

# R

1 **Rabbet** Channel of wood
*The **rabbet** beside this door is beautifully carved.*
**Rabbit** An animal
Have you heard the story of **rabbit** and tortoise?

2 **Race** Competition
*Who won the 100 mt. **race**?*
**Raise** To lift
Students will **raise** their hands for attendance.
**Rays** That throws light
The **rays** of the sun are sharp.
**Raze** Destroy
The building was **razed** within no time.

3 **Rack** For holding things
*Some useful books for you are in that **rack**.*
**Rake** Dissolute man of fashion
The **rake** was severely punished by the police for his misbehaviour.
**Reckless** Care
I cannot afford to be **reckless** about my career.
**Wreak** Revenge
What good will come of **wreak**?
**Wreck** Destroy
"Titanic" was **wrecked** in mid-sea.

4 **Radial** Of rays

*The **radial** effect on skin is sometimes harmful.*

**Redial** Connect phone again

You can **redial** this number and call him.

5 **Radical** Fundamental

*Many **radical** changes are needed in our social system.*

**Radical** Small root

Dig out the **radical** of this plant.

6 **Radish** A vegetable

*I do not prefer **radish** in salad.*

**Reddish** Little red

She is wearing a **reddish** saree.

7 **Raid** Sudden attack

*The army **raided** the hut to catch the terrorists.*

**Red** A colour

**Red** signal says "Stop".

8 **Rain** Fall of water from sky

*How was the **rain** last monsoon?*

**Reign** Rule

There was peace and prosperity during the **reign** of Lord Ram.

**Rein** Bridle

Hold tight the **rein** of this stallion.

9 **Rant** Make noise

*There was a lot of **rant** in the boy's hostel yesterday evening.*

**Rent** Amount of hire

What is the **rent** of this house?

10 **Rare** Happening sometimes

***Rare** species of animals should be protected.*

**Rear** Back part

The **rear** wheel of my car is punctured.

11 **Rash** Rough mannered

*His son is very **rash**.*

**Rush** Crowd

There was a **rush** for shopping during Diwali.

12 **Rat** Mouse

***Rat** is afraid of cat.*

**Rate** Price

The **rate** of this furniture is very high.

13 **Raw** Uncooked

*We don't eat **raw** food.*

**Row** Line

Soldiers are standing in a **row** for parade.

14 **Reach** Be there

*When will you **reach** Mumbai?*

**Rich** Wealthy

The **rich** should not be proud.

15 **Read** Go through words

*Do you **read** magazine regularly?*

**Reed** Water plant

The pond should be cleared of **reeds**.

**Rid** Avoid

How will you get **rid** of this pestering visitor?

16 **Ready** Prepared
*Are you **ready** for your performance?*
**Reedy** Full of reeds
*We cannot swim in this **reedy** lake.*

17 **Recourse** Resort to
*I can **recourse** on my knowledge and wisdom.*
**Resource** Means
India has many natural **resources**.

18 **Reel** Cylindrical device
*Please use a red **reel** to stitch my coat.*
**Rill** Small stream
The bath in the **rill** was very refreshing.

19 **Refuge** Shelter
*India has given **refuge** to many helpless people.*
**Refuse** Not to accept
You can't **refuse** my entry.

20 **Regal** Fit for monarch
*It was **regal** function in the palace ground.*
**Regale** Entertain
Our boss likes to **regale** the staff members on all good occasions.

21 **Relay** Convey
*The programme will be **relayed** through satellite.*
**Rely** Trust
I can **rely** on my best friend.

22 **Remainder** Which is left
*You can throw away the **remainder** of lunch.*
**Reminder** To remind
Please send them the **reminder** for payment.

23 **Repeal** Revoke
*The bill will **repeal** from the parliament.*
**Repel** Drive back
The lion **repelled** on seeing the elephant.

24 **Repress** Crush
*I **repressed** my sad feeling and enjoyed with others.*
**Re-price** Price again
It is necessary to **re-price** these goods.
**Reprise** Repeat item
The audience is asking for **reprise** of this song.

25 **Rest** Refresh
*We should take sufficient **rest** after hard work.*
**Wrest** Snatch
Why did you **wrest** book from my hand?

26 **Retail** Sell in small quantity
*What is the **retail** price of this medicine?*
**Retell** Tell again
I will **retell** the story for you.

27 **Reveal** Disclose
*He did not **reveal** his identity to us.*
**Revel** Make merry
We **revel** in festival.

28 **Revere** Deep respect
*All Indians **revere** Gandhiji.*
**Reverie** Day dreaming
His habit of **reverie** is not good.

29 **Review** Critique of book
*Have you read the **review** of the latest books?*
**Revue** Satirical play
They are presenting a **revue** tonight.

30 **Rice** A grain
*Boil the **rice**.*
**Rise** Get up
There was a sudden **rise** in gold price.

31 **Right** Just and proper
*Your answer is **right**.*
**Rite** Ceremonies
The marriage **rite** will take place in temple.
**Write** Note down
Please, **write** your name here.

32 **Ring** Ornament
*I like diamond studded **rings**.*
**Wring** Squeeze
**Wring** it with all your might.

33 **Road** Path
*Drive carefully along the **M.G Road**.*
**Rod** Thin pole
Fix this **rod** in the machine.
**Rode** Past tense of ride
They **rode** on camel in desert.

34 **Rob** Loot
*How did they **rob** the bank?*
**Robe** Loose dress
Your **robe** needs good stitching.

35 **Role** Part
*Sardar Patel played a major **role** in uniting India.*
**Roll** Register
*Your name is out of the **payroll**.*

36 **Root** Origin

*Population is the **root** of all problems in India.*

**Rout** Complete defeat

The rebels were **routed** by the army.

**Route** Path

Which is the **route** to airport?

37 **Rung** Bell of telephone

*The peon has **rung** the bell.*

**Wrung** Squeezed

She has not **wrung** the clothes properly.

❑

# S

1 **Sack** Large bag
*Wheat is packed in **sack**.*
**Sake** Because of
He did the work for my **sake**.

2 **Sail** Travel in ship
*'Unicorn' will **sail** in the Atlantic.*
**Sale** Conduct sell
There is a **sale** of antiques in the town hall.
**Sell** Give for money
He **sells** fruit.

3 **Sallow** A willow plant
*Some **sallows** have grown in the forest.*
**Shallow** Not deep
Don't be afraid, the water is **shallow**.

4 **Same** Similar
*We use **same** brand of watches.*
**Shame** Embarrass
It is not a **shame** to be born poor.

5 **Sanctity** Holiness
*We should maintain the **sanctity** of holy places.*
**Sanctify** Treat as holy
Priests are considered as **sanctified**.

6 **Sand** Dry mud
*Do you like to build **sand** castles?*
**Send** Dispatch to
I will **send** him some money.

7 **Sat** To sit (past tense)
*He **sat** beside me.*
**Sate** Gratify
Take this food and **sate** your hunger.
**Set** Pair, group
This **sofa set** is expensive.

8 **Saviour** One who saves
*Is the world waiting for a **saviour**?*
**Savour** Flavour
Who does not like sweet **savour**?

9 **Saw** See (past tense)
*I **saw** the film with interest.*
**Sew** Stitch
Can you **sew** a coat?
**So** That is why
He is late, **so** he is driving fast.
**Sow** To plant seeds
What did you **sow** in your farm?

10 **Scam** Fraud
*He was caught in a bank **scam**.*
**Scan** Look intently
The custom officer **scanned** my bag.

11 **Scar** Mark of injury
*How did he get a **scar** on the face?*
**Scare** To frighten
Don't **scare** the child.

12 **Scene** Spectacle
*The state of Himachal Pradesh has some beautiful natural **scenes**.*
**Seen** See (participle)
Have **seen** Leaning Tower of Pizza?

13 **Sceptic** Unbeliever in religion
*He won't come to the temple, he is a **sceptic**.*
**Septic** Putrefying
You should take injection before **septic** happens.

14 **Scoop** Big spoon
*I will have two **scoops** of ice-cream.*
**Scope** Opportunity
There is much **scope** for Indian youths in the field of computers.

15 **Scour** Clean
*You should **scour** the dishes.*
**Score** Number of points
What is the **score** of our team?

16 **Scrawl** Write fast
*The secretary **scrawled** what the boss said.*
**Scroll** Roll of paper
Fix this **scroll** into the printer.

17 **Sea** Ocean
*India is surrounded by **sea** on three sides.*
**See** Look
Can you **see** that signpost?

18 **Seam** Joint
*The pipeline is out at **seam**.*
**Seem** Looks
You **seem** worried.

19 **Seat** Place to sit
*What is your **seat** number?*
**Sit** Act of sitting
**Sit** in the front row.

20 **Secret** Hidden
*Army **secret** should not be leaked.*
**Secrete** Discharge
Doctor will **secrete** the bad blood.

21 **Seek** Search
*He has gone out of country to **seek** fortune.*
**Sick** Ill
He is very **sick**.

22 **Self** Own self
*I will do this work **myself**.*
**Shelf** Rake
The books are arranged on a **shelf**.

23 **Sensual** Physical
*Is marriage meant only for **sensual** pleasures?*
**Sensuous** Affecting senses
Keats wrote **sensuous** poetry.

24 **Serf** Oppressed worker
*Landlords had many **serfs**.*
**Surf** Foam of sea
The beach is full of **surf**.

25 **Sever** Divide
*Father will **sever** the property between two brothers.*
**Severe** Harsh
There should be **severe** punishment to traitors.

26 **Shade** Shelter
*Park your car under the **shade** of tree.*
**Shed** Let fall of
Snake **sheds** its skin.

27 **Shall** To show future
*I **shall** complete the task.*
**Shale** A slate stone
We can write with chalk on **shale**.

28 **Shear** Cut
*The cobbler will **shear** the leather.*
**Sheer** Complete
There was **sheer** enjoyment in function.

29 **Sheet** Large rectangle piece
*Many **sheets** of iron are stored in the warehouse.*
**Shit** Show anger
**Shit**! I have made the same mistake.

30 **Sheep** An animal
*Marino **sheep** of Australia gives good wool.*
**Ship** Large boat
Overseas transportation is carried out by **ship**.

31 **Shift** Change position
*We have **shifted** our house.*
**Sift** Pass through sieve
This grain must be **sifted**.

32 **Short** Not long
*Your pant is **short**.*
**Sort** Kind
What **sort** of language is that?

33 **Simulate** Pretend
*He will **simulate** ... he children.*
**Stimulate**
Your misbehaviour will **stimulate** his anger.

34 **Slate** Rock used for writing
*... tes were distributed among children in school.*
**Slat** Narrow piece
It is difficult to punch hole in this wooden **slat**.

35 **Sleek** Smooth and glossy
*These bangles are **sleek**.*
**Slick** Skilful
**Slick** people are in demand.

36 **Sleep** Rest with eyes closed
***Sleep** gives rest to body and mind.*
**Slip** Fall
How did your bike **slip**?

37 **Sleet** Snow and rain
*We experienced **sleet** when we had gone for trekking.*
**Slit** Cut into strips
Please **slit** this card for me.

38 **Small** Little
*His house is too **small** for four persons.*
**Smell** Fragrance
Do you like the **smell** of rose?

39 **Snack** Food
*What will you have in **snack**?*
**Snake** A reptile
Beware, that **snake** is poisonous.

40 **Sneak** Move unobserved
*The thief was caught **sneaking** around the bank.*
**Snick** Make small notch
I will carve a **snick** on the wall.

41 **Soak** Make wet
*I am **soaked** in rain.*
**Sock** Undergarment of feet
My **socks** need a wash.

42 **Soap** Bathing material
*Which **soap** do you use?*
**Sop** Thing given for bribe
They gave cash for **sop**.

43 **Soar** Fly
*Some birds can **soar** till great height.*
**Sore** Causing pain
I have a **sore** throat.

44 **Sole** Bottom of shoe
*Shoes should have strong **sole**.*
**Soul** Spirit of person
We should have pure **soul**.

45 **Some** Not few or many
*Give me **some** water.*
**Sum** Total
What is the **sum** of your calculation?

46 **Some time** Duration of time
*It will take me **some time** to recover from illness.*
**Sometimes** On occasions
I like to sit idle **sometimes**.

47 **Son** Male child
*He has two **sons**.*
**Sun** A Star
Life is impossible without **sun**.

48 **Sooth** Truth
*The **sooth** sayer predicted a great fortune.*
**Soothe** Calm
This medicine will **soothe** your mind.

49 **Spacious** Much space
*Your new house is very **spacious**.*
**Specious** Attractive
His point of view, though **specious**, is not worth considering.

50 **Spade** Garden instrument
*Dig with a **spade**.*
**Sped** Fast
He **sped** on the bike.

51 **Spar** Crystalline mineral
*Do you know the uses of **spar**?*
**Spare** Let go
I will **spare** you this time.

52 **Spat** Part of shoe
*The cobbler wills mend the **spat**.*
**Spate** River-flood
The **spate** will cause much destruction.

53 **Spec** Speculation
*So much of **spec** is going on in the stock market.*
**Speck** Stain
How will you remove the **speck** of tea from your shirt?

54 **Spear** Pointed weapon
*Masai people of Africa use **spear** to hunt.*
**Sphere** A shape
Earth is a very big **sphere**.

55 **Spectacle** Scene
*The **spectacle** from above the mountain is wonderful.*
**Spectacles** Optical
Who is that lady with dark **spectacles**?

56 **Spice** Eatables
*India is famous for **spices**.*
**Spies** Detectives
Enemy countries send many **spies** to India.

57 **Spilt** Pour accidentally
*Who has **spilt** water on the floor?*
**Split** Divide
You can **split** the paper for writing notes.

58 **Spit** Throw saliva
*Don't **spit** here.*
**Spite** Malice
Why does he **spite** me?

59 **Stag** Big deer
*The **stag** vanished in the bushes on seeing us.*
**Stage** Raised platform
This is my first performance on the **stage**.

60 **Stair** Steps
*You have to climb twenty **stairs** to reach the terrace.*
**Stare** Look constantly
Why is that man **staring** at me?

61 **Stalk** Stem

*The **stalk** of this plant is very tall and thick.*

**Stock** Big quantity

We have a big **stock** of cloth in our shop.

62 **Stall** Temporary store

*There are many food **stalls** over there.*

**Stole** Steal (past tense)

Who **stole** your watch?

63 **Stationary** Not moving

*Mountains are **stationary** objects.*

**Stationery** Writing materials

I would like to buy some **stationery** for office.

64 **Statue** Carved image

*How beautiful is this **statue** carved!*

**Statute** Law

What does the **statute** say about this matter?

65 **Stay** Remain

*I will **stay** in Mumbai till Sunday.*

**Sty** Illness of eye

Doctor has prescribed an eye-drop for **sty**.

66 **Steak** Slice

*Throw the **steak** into the cage of lion.*

**Stick** Wooden rod

Shepherds use **stick** to drive cattle.

67 **Steal** Take away unknown

*Anybody can **steal** your ornaments if you don't take care.*

**Steel** A metal

**Steel** is a widely used metal.

**Still** Not moving

Stand-**still**, I am clicking.

68 **Stimulant** Intoxicating

*Whisky is a strong **stimulant**.*

**Stimulus** Encouragement

The declaration of bonus proved a great **stimulus** to the workers.

69 **Storey** Division of house

*On which **storey** is your flat?*

**Story** Tale

The teacher told an interesting **story**.

70 **Straight** Not curved

*Draw a **straight** line on this paper.*

**Strait** Narrow

This gate is very **strait**.

71 **Strip** Remove clothes

***Strip** the baby before bath.*

**Stripe** Piece of land

We have grown vegetables on that **stripe**.

72 **Suit** Action in court

*I filed a **suit** against his company.*

**Suite** A set of rooms

I like to live in luxury **suite**.

**Soot** Black substance in smoke

How do you use lamp **soot**?

73 **Sundae** Ice-cream with fruits

*I would like to have a **sundae** after dinner.*

**Sunday** First day of week

**Sunday** is a holiday.

74 **Super** Excellent
*Have you heard the story of* ***Superman****?*
**Supper** Late evening meal
I had a light **supper**.

75 **Superficial** Lacking depth
*His* ***superficial*** *sincerity did not create any feelings in me.*
**Superfluous** Useless
You must cut the **superfluous** expenses in your household budget.

76 **Surely** Certainly
*He will* ***surely*** *help us.*
**Surly** Bad tempered
His father has a **surly** nature.

77 **Sweat** Perspiration
*I* ***sweat*** *after running.*
**Sweet** A taste
This mango is **sweet**.

❑

# T

1 **Tail** Part of animal's body

*The elephant has a short **tail**.*

**Tale** Story

Grandma told me a fairy **tale**.

**Tell** Say

I will **tell** you about my life.

2 **Tall** Good in height

*Giraffe is very **tall**.*

**Toll** Tax

Who is collecting the **toll** here?

3 **Tamper** Interfere with

*Do not **tamper** the project report, it is illegal.*

**Temper** Temperament

You should have controlled your **temper** in presence of many people.

**Tempera** Method of painting using an enulsion

Italian painters use **tempera** method for painting.

4 **Tan** Yellowish-brown colour

*The cobbler will apply **tan** on the leather.*

**Ten** A digit

There are **ten** members in our family.

5 **Tap** From where water comes
*Put the bucket under the **tap**.*
**Tape** Instrument for playing music
Insert this cassette in the **tape**.

6 **Tare** Food for cattle
*The cows are given enough **tare** in our field.*
**Tear** Cut
Don't **tear** this letter.

7 **Tarry** Stay
*I will **tarry** here for two minutes.*
**Terry** Fabric for towels
This is a fine **terry** towel.

8 **Taste** Feeling on tongue
*How is the **taste** of this biscuit?*
**Test** Exam
How many marks did you get in the **test**?

9 **Taught** Teach, train
*Who **taught** you English?*
**Tot** Small child
Whose **tot** is this?

10 **Taut** Tight
*It is a very **taut** seat.*
**Tout** One who finds customers
That young **tout** has done a good job.

11 **Tea** A drink
*Most people like **tea**.*
**Tee** Article of golf
The player is examining the **tee**.

12 **Team** A company

*Indian cricket **team** is very good.*

**Teem** Full of

This glass **teems** with milk.

13 **Tenant** One who rents

*How much rent do you charge from your **tenant**?*

**Tenet** Principle

You have to follow the **tenets** in school.

14 **Than** Compared with

*India is bigger **than** Pakistan.*

**Then** Thereafter

I arrange my table **then** I start my work.

15 **Their** Belonging to them

*That is **their** house.*

**There** At that place

I went **there** to find some news.

16 **Third** Number three in rank

*I stood **third** in the university exam.*

**Thud** Sound after falling

Branch fell with a **thud** on ground.

17 **Thresh** Separate grain from corn

*We will **thresh** the grains very soon.*

**Thrash** Beat

Don't **thrash** him cruelly.

18 **Throne** Ruler's seat

*Shahjahan had made the Peacock **Throne**.*

**Thrown** Hurl

Haven't you **thrown** the ball yet?

19 **Throw** Hurl

*Don't **throw** the watch.*

**Throe** Violent pang

He is undergoing **throe** in his head.

20 **Tic** Contraction of muscle

*The doctor is explaining about the **tic**.*

**Tick** Insect

Our dog has got many **ticks**.

21 **Tiddly** Slightly drunk

*He won't drive he is **tiddly**.*

**Tidily** Neatly

How **tidily** you keep your room!

22 **Tier** Arrange on each other

*This is a three **tier** train.*

**Tire** To be exhausted

When he tires of writing, he listens music.

**Tyre** Rubber wheel

My car needs a new **tyre**.

23 **Tilt** Slanted

*Why is this scooter **tilted**?*

**Tilth** Cultivation

There is **tilth** of cotton plants in our farm.

24 **Ting** Sound of bell

*Where did the **ting** sound come from?*

**Tinge** Slight effect

There is a **tinge** of madness in great scholars.

25 **To** A preposition
*I am talking **to** you.*
**Too** Much
Your house is **too** far.
**Two** A digit
He has **two** daughters.

26 **Toe** Part of foot
*These shoes are tight at the **toe**.*
**Tow** Pull
The ship had to be **towed** till the port.

27 **Ton** Unit of weight
*How many **tons** does an adult elephant weigh?*
**Tone** Strengthen, manner of speaking
He was in cheerful **tone**.
This capsule will **tone** your muscles.
**Tun** Cask of wine beer
The **tun** was emptied in the celebration.

28 **Tongs** Article for holding
*You can use **tongs** to hold hot bread.*
**Tongue** Part inside the mouth
"Show me your **tongue**," said the doctor.

29 **Top** Foremost
*I am at the **top** in my class.*
**Tope** Drink excess
He is **toped** after the party.

30 **Tore** Cut
*Who **tore** my letter?*
**Torr** Unit of pressure
Tell me the **torr** reading.

31 **Tortuous** Twisted
*I don't need this **tortuous** bar.*
**Torturous** Painful
That accident was a very **torturous** experience.

32 **Tosh** Nonsense
*I don't like your **tosh** words.*
**Toss** Throw up
I will **toss** the ball, you catch it.

33 **Tough** Strong
*My brother has become a **tough** man after joining the Army.*
**Tuff** Rock from ash
Geologists are working on **tuff**.

34 **Track** Path
*The railway **track** is made of iron bars.*
**Trek** Travel by walking
I like to **trek** in cool and peaceful atmosphere.

35 **Trade** Carry out business
*We **trade** in chemicals.*
**Tread** Walk
**Tread** slowly with me.

36 **Trail** Beaten path
*We can find animal **trails** in jungle.*
**Trill** Rapid sound
The trumpet **trills** very loudly.

37 **Trip** Excursion
*We have arranged a **trip** to Goa.*
**Tripe** Belly of animal
Many animals rest on **tripe**.

38 **Travail** Pain of childbirth

*It was difficult for her to bear the **travail**.*

**Travel** Passage

I like to **travel** by train.

39 **Twin** Closely related pair

*Tina and Mina are **twin** sisters.*

**Twine** Coarse string

Only **twine** can hold this bundle tightly.

❑

## U

1 **Unit** Standard

*What is the **unit** for measuring the intensity of an earthquake?*

**Unite** Get together

Sardar Patel **united** all the states in to one country.

2 **Urban** Related to city

*Urban legend is ahat everyone knows them.*

**Urbane** Stylish

He is very **urbane** in conversation.

# V

1 **Vacation** Holidays

*Where will you during this **vacation**?*

**Vocation** Profession

He is a teacher by **vocation**.

2 **Vain** Useless

*You should stop your **vain** efforts.*

**Vane** Blade of a windmill

The windmill has large **vanes**.

**Vein** Part of body

**Veins** are very important in our body.

**Wane** Decrease in size and time

How can we **wane** our wastage in factory?

**When** Inquire or inform about time

**When** shall we meet?

3 **Vale** Valley

*At night the **vale** seems monstrous.*

**Wale** Injury from whip or rod

The horse has a **wale** on back.

**Well** Good

She sings **well**.

**Whale** Largest fish

**Whale** is a friendly fish.

4 **Valet** Personal servant

*My **valet** is very honest and sincere.*

**Wallet** Male purse

He keeps his wife's photograph in his **wallet**.

5 **Valley** Gorge

*Kashmir **valley** is a beautiful part of India.*

**Wally** Foolish

Your **wally** servant has made a terrible mistake.

6 **Valour** Bravery

*There are many tales of Arjun's **valour**.*

**Velour** A fabric

This cloth is made of **velour**.

7 **Van** Long car

*Milk is delivered in **van**.*

**Wan** Pale

The colour on the wall seems **wan**.

8 **Variable** Changeable

*Is the result of this process **variable**?*

**Veritable** Rightly called

Your brother is a **veritable** genius.

9 **Variety** Many sidedness

*You will find good **variety** of garments in our showroom.*

**Verity** Fundamental truth

Death is a **verity** of human life.

10 **Vary** Differ

*The observation of this experiment **varies**.*

**Very** Much

Russia is a **very** big country.

**Wary** Cautious

**Wary** persons face less trouble.

**Weary** Tired

They will **weary** after such a long walk.

11 **Vas** A vessel

*What is in that **vas**?*

**Vase** Article to keep flowers

They presented me a **vase** for my new office.

12 **Vault** Jump with the help of bamboo

*Soldiers play **vaulting** in free time.*

**Volt** Unit of electricity

How many **volts** does this gadget consume?

13 **Veer** Change direction

*The captain will **veer** ship smoothly.*

**Wear** Put on

What will you **wear** in the annual function?

14 **Veil** Cover

*Bridegroom's face is covered by **veil**.*

**Wail** Weep

Why is the little boy **wailing**?

15 **Veld** — Open country

*There is plenty o ... ttle in the **veld**.*

**Weld** — ...ating

Please, **weld** this machine parts together.

**Wield** — Hold and use weapon

The knight **wields** his sword on the tiger.

16 **Venal** — Bribery

*What did that man offer as **venal**?*

**Venial** — Pardonable

His crime is not **venial**.

17 **Vent** — Outlet

*He shouted and gave **vent** to his anger.*

**Went** — Past of go

They **went** to Mumbai yesterday.

18 **Verse** — Poem

*Shakespeare wrote some great **verses**.*

**Worse** — Very bad

Drinking is **worse** than smoking.

19 **Vest** — Undergarments

*I have a comfortable **vest**.*

**Waist** — A part of body

What is your **waist** size?

**Waste** — To spoil

We should not **waste** water.

20 **Vex** — Irritate

*If you **vex** me now, I will hit you.*

**Wax** — Material used to make candle

**Wax** melts fast.

21 **Vice** Bad habit

*We must keep away from **vices**.*

**Wise** Clever

Our teacher is a **wise** man.

22 **Vile** Mean

*He is a very **vile** man.*

**Wile** Trick

I will use a **wile** to appease them.

**While** Space of time

I met her **while** I was in college.

23 **Villain** Bad person

*I liked the role of **villain** in this film.*

**Villein** Feudal tenant

How much do you pay your **villeins**?

24 **Vine** Plant of grapes

*Do you know that story of fox who could not reach the **vine**?*

**Wine** Alcoholic drink

I would like to take red **wine**.

25 **Vintner** Vine-merchant

*The **vintner** made good profit in the season.*

**Winter** Cold-season

**Winter** is cold but good season.

26 **Violate** Break the law

*You will be fined if you **violate** traffic rules.*

**Violet** A colour

**Violet** is one of the colours in the rainbow.

27 **Violation** Infringe

*What result came out of such **violation**?*

**Violence** Force

Gandhiji never believed in **violence**.

28 **Viscose** Cellulose

*What are the uses of **viscose**?*

**Viscous** Sticky

Gum is a **viscous** material.

29 **Vole** Rat like animal

*Is that **vole** or rat?*

**Wall** Concrete structure for partition

The compound **wall** is very high.

30 **Vote** Expression of choice

*We should **vote** for good candidates.*

**Watt** Unit of electricity

How can you measure **watt** of this appliance?

**What** Asking, inquiring

**What** is his name?

31 **Voter** One who votes

*How many **voters** are in this village?*

**Water** A liquid

We must drink good amount of **water**.

32 **Vow** Promise

*Our brave soldiers have taken a **vow** to protect our country.*

**Wow** Show surprise

**Wow**! What an unexpected luck!

❑

# W

1 **Wad** — Lump of soft material used to block hole

*A **wad** was put at the hole to keep away rats.*

**Wade** — Walk in water

You find many people **wading** on beach.

**Wed** — To marry

He **wedded** last month.

2 **Waif** — An abandoned child

*The **waif** was brought up in an orphanage.*

**Wife** — Spouse (female)

My **wife** is a perfect life partner.

3 **Wait** — Be expectant

*I will **wait** for you till 10.00 p.m.*

**Weight** — Heaviness

How much is the **weight** of your bag?

4 **Waive** — Give up

*I have **waived** my job to start my own business.*

**Wave** — Move

I **waved** hand to my friend.

**Waves** are rising in sea.

5 **Wand** Stick used by magician
*The magician raised his **wand** to show the trick.*
**Wend** Make one's way
He **wended** through the crowd.

6 **Wander** Walk aimlessly
*It is nice to **wander** about.*
**Wonder** Surprise
I **wonder** why he did it.

7 **Want** Need
*Do you **want** anything?*
**Won't** Not to become
I **won't** be late for the meeting.

8 **Ward** Part of building
*I live in the left **ward**.*
**Word** An element of speech
You have good **word** power.

9 **Ware** Goods for sale
*I am searching some good item from the **ware**.*
**Wear** To put on
He likes to **wear** T-shirt and jeans.

10 **Warm** Little hot
*I will take some **warm** tea.*
**Worm** An insect
**Worms** are useful for soil.

11 **We** A pronoun
***We** are students of literature.*
**Wee** Small in size
I just want a **wee** slice of bread.

12 **Weak** Not strong

*You have become **weak** after sickness.*

**Week** Period of seven days

I will be in Kolkata next **week**.

**Wick** Part of lamp

Submerge the **wick** in oil.

13 **Weal** Welfare

*What steps does the government take for **weal** of people?*

**Will** Verb

He **will** be a good citizen.

**Wheel** Ring that gives motion to vehicle

The **wheel** of my cart is of iron.

14 **Wean** Accustom an infant to food other *than mother's milk*

It is time to **wean** this child.

**Win** Be victor

We can **win** this match if we perform well.

15 **Weather** Season

*The **weather** here is very pleasant.*

**Whether** If

Tell me **whether** he will join us or not.

16 **Wet** Soaked

*How did you get **wet**?*

**Whet** Sharpen

Please, **whet** the point of my pencil.

17 **Which** Asking for choice

***Which** colour do you like?*

**Witch** Woman with devil spirits

People believed in **witch** power long ago.

18 **Whither** Where
***Whither** can you find such a peaceful place?*
**Wither** To fade
This rose will **wither** soon.

19 **Whore** Prostitute
*Police is keeping a watch on the **whore**.*
**Wore** Past tense of wear
He **wore** a coat yesterday.

20 **With** Means or company used
*I write **with** left hand.*
**With** Tough flexible shoot
The shepherd uses **with** to drive cattle.

21 **Wood** Substance of tree
***Wooden** furniture has become costly.*
**Would** Express condition
I **would** like to come with you.

22 **Write** To note down
*I **write** many letters from my office.*
**Writ** Written command
The High Court has issued a **writ**.

❑

# Y

1 **Yarn** Spun thread

*We make **yarns** in our factory.*

**Yearn** To long for

The old lady **yearns** to see her grandchildren.

2 **Yoke** Bondage

*I have **yoked** the bullocks in the cart.*

**Yolk** Yellow part of the egg

**Yolk** tasted bitter today.

3 **Yore** Long time ago

*In times of **yore,** people travelled by horses and carts.*

**Your** Belonging to you

Where is **your** house?

❑❑❑